Christian Revival
for
Israel's Survival

Victor Mordecai

July 1999

Book Cover: The book's cover is comprised of the title "Christian Revival for Israel's Survival," and the flags of Israel and the USA because it is Christian America, God's most chosen country that must come to the defense of Israel, God's chosen nation. The circular emblem of St. George killing the dragon is representative of Judeo-Christianity vanquishing the dragon of Islam. I refer to this in the book with verses from Revelation chapters 12 and 17. The words in Cyrillic letters say: Moscow is the heart of Russia. The reason for using this symbol is that the Christian revival, I believe is necessary for the defense of Israel, the West and the entire world, must encompass the Eastern Orthodox Churches as well. This includes, among others, the Coptic, Ethiopian, Greek, Bulgarian, Serbian, Romanian, and, of course Russian and Ukrainian Orthodox Churches for they are threatened by the global domination of Islam just as the Protestant and Catholic Churches are threatened. St. George killing the dragon is often seen in these Eastern Orthodox areas as representing precisely that — the victory of Judeo-Christianity over Islam. Christian Revival for Israel's Survival must include all Christian believers to succeed.

First Printing - July, 1999
Taylors, South Carolina
10,000 copies - 162 pages

Table of Contents

Direct inquiries to:

Victor Mordecai
PO Box 18209
Jerusalem, Israel 91181
Fax: 011 972 2 629 0574 Ext. 7157

For reordering this book in the U.S.
1-800-540-0828

Preface

Ever since writing the first edition of my first book "Is Fanatic Islam a Global Threat?" in January 1995, I have encountered a never-ending flow of information confirming and even reinforcing my message that Islam's agenda is world domination and therefore a global threat. My book has grown from a mere 60 page pamphlet in its first printing to 93 pages in its second printing in May 1995, to 170 pages in the third edition in February 1996, to 200 pages in the fourth edition in May 1996, and finally 286 pages in the fifth and final edition in December 1997.

I was really rather tired of constantly updating, reediting and compiling each new edition, so I decided not to reopen the text. Enough was enough. Well, a year and half has gone by since edition V of my first book. Not only has new information accumulated in an avalanche too serious to ignore, but the threat of the Islamic agenda has now been joined by the threat of another agenda - that of the one world government, the globalists, the bankers, whatever one wants to call them.

It is true that much is mentioned in my previous book about the globalist agenda, but my inescapable conclusions of the last year and a half is that the combined Islamic-globalist threat is as dangerous as a binary chemical weapon on the battlefield is dangerous, maybe even more so.

At this point, I feel it incumbent upon me to relate again an experience that shook my life and made me realize why a Judeo-Christian alliance is an imperative. I will try not to repeat too much of the material appearing in my first book here in my second book. But my confrontation with the Dallas Council on World Affairs on April 14th, 1991 was to teach me a lesson that needs to be repeated in this book as well.

I was invited to speak before the Dallas Council on World Affairs, just weeks after the conclusion of Operation Desert Storm. Now, I had not realized it at that time, but the this organization was a local branch of an organization affiliated with the Council on Foreign Relations based in New York City.

Whereas in the past, I spoke usually only in churches and synagogues, this was my first secular forum. It was a bankers' and petrodollar forum. It was the monied people of Dallas who were hosting me this time, not Bible people.

Since this speaking appearance took place while the Likud administration of Yitzhak Shamir was still in office, I had to take the brunt of some heavy criticism by the Dallas Council people who were very unhappy with Shamir and the Likud Party's "intransigent" position.

It must be remembered that Israel was the unsung hero of Desert Storm. In spite of being hit with a barrage of 39 Iraqi scud missiles, Israel held its fire and did not counterattack against Iraq, exactly as the US-Arab coalition of allies instructed Israel. Yet Israel has always "been there" for the US if so needed as a land-based "aircraft carrier," a logistical pre-positioning station, or a second line of defense for the US and the West throughout the Cold War period as well as after. I was not prepared for the rough "broadside" with which I was about to be bombarded by the Dallas Council people.

The main thrust of my message that night was very politically correct from a quasi-Israeli government spokesman. It should be remembered that it was the administration of Prime Minister Yitzhak Shamir that initiated the Madrid Peace Talks of 1990, with Benjamin Netanyahu leading the Israeli delegation.

I explained in my lecture that Israel had already complied 93% with UN Resolutions 242 and 338 calling for Israeli withdrawal from territories taken during the 1967 and 1973 wars by returning all of Sinai to Egypt (91%) and half of the Golan (2%) to Syria. The remaining 7% of the territories (Judea, Samaria, Gaza and the other half of the Golan Heights) should remain with Israel, because Israel had already compromised 93%, and these few remaining territories were vital to Israel's defense.

In addition, it should be remembered that the two UN resolutions do not call for a full withdrawal from all territories taken by Israel in wars of self-defense in 1967 and 1973. On the contrary, it calls for negotiations between Israel and its neighbors for secure, recognized and defensible new boundaries, because even former Israeli foreign minister Abba Eban had called the 1967 armistice lines "Auschwitz Lines" because they were indefensible. Had the UN meant total withdrawal, it would have said so. Had the UN meant total withdrawal, there would not have been any room for words "negotiations for secure, recognized and defensible borders."

After I finish speaking, we adjourned to dinner, to be followed later by a closed meeting, during which questions would be asked of me.

During that question and answer period, I was dealt one of the harshest experiences of my life. I was basically told that in spite of being born and educated as an American, and as a result was an eloquent spokesman for Israel, I had to be "taught" the "realities" of life or realpolitik.

The first reality was as follows: "America is tired of paying for Israel's wars. Israel will pay whatever price it must to make peace with its Arab neighbors. In other words, Israel must fully capitulate to the Arabs and return all the territories it was forced to take in 1967 and 1973, including Eastern Jerusalem, disregarding UN resolutions 242 and 338, because the US would no longer stand by Israel. Israel was completely alone, and the US was no longer to be considered an ally.

The second reality was as follows: "The only thing that made America great was the barrel of oil, the steady price of oil and the steady supply of oil, and we (the US) will not let Israel and the Jews stand as an obstacle to steady oil prices and supplies."

Now, before I could answer them, two Christian evangelical couples which had arranged for me to be invited to appear on Marlin Maddoux's radio program as well as Zola Levitt's "Holy Land Program" both out of Dallas, and who were now my guests at this dinner and lecture I gave, asked permission to address the Dallas Council people.

One of them, a Mr. Eric Gustavson, got up, shaking with fury, and said: "You should all be ashamed of yourselves. You call yourselves Christians? What made America great was not the barrel of oil, but Jesus Christ!" and he said down. Then his daughter arose and added: "Besides, it says in the Bible '*Whoever blesses Israel is blessed, and whoever curses Israel is cursed.*'" (Genesis 27:29 and Numbers 24:9)

Then it was my turn. My reply to the Dallas Council on World Affairs was as follows: "We Jews have been around 4,000 years. We are a stiff-necked, rambunctious, and rebellious people. God punished us again and again for our failing to fulfill God's commandments as we had agreed to do in Exodus 19:5. Only a remnant of the Jewish people remains today. But we do remain because God made a promise to us. Also, Israel was resurrected from the ash heap of history after 2,000 years of Jewish Diaspora. Whether we deserved it or not is a moot point. What matters is that God and biblical prophecy called for the return of the Jews to the Holy Land and for the recreation and resurrection of the Jewish State a third time. This is scriptural.

Now oil reserves will run out some time during the coming century, perhaps in 60 or 70 years. Or an alternative energy source will be found. Until that time happens, we Jews will not sacrifice ourselves and 4,000 years of our existence for sixty more years of steady oil prices and oil supplies. It is enough that we paid six million Jews as a price for the petrodollar-Arab pressures on England and the US to slam shut the doors of emigration to the Jews of Europe by not allowing them to go to Palestine or virtually anywhere else in the 20's and 30's, thus leaving them prey to the Nazi satanic Holocaust. So the Jews have already paid the price for steady oil prices and supplies. We will not pay with yet another five million Jews from Israel so that the oil corporations will be pleased. Sorry!

But the importance of that night in my life was not in what I said, but what I heard and learned that the Jews were the sacrifice on the altar of oil. That the Jews had no friends, except perhaps for Bible Christians. Mr. Gustavson and his daughter were my allies that night, but we were the minority in that room.

I saw in 1991, and even more so today in 1999, I see a battlefield in front of me. My four evangelical Christian friends represented Christian America and the other twenty or so people in the room of the Dallas Council on Foreign Affairs represented the anti-Christ or anti-Christian America. The battlefield, at this stage, was controlled by the victorious armies of mammon (money) while the Christians were weak, ineffectual and disorganized.

To quote from the Gospel of Luke 16:13: *No servant can serve two masters: for either he will hate the one and love the other; or else he will hold to the one and despise the other. Ye cannot serve God and mammon.*

It was that night, on the 14th of April, 1991, that I, an Israeli, a Jew, and an officer in the Israel Defense Forces reserves, came to the conclusion that for God's sake, for the sake of Israel, for the sake of all Jews, I would devote my future efforts to promoting the cause of the Christian side as opposed to the anti-Christ side that would acquiesce to and maybe even support another Jewish Holocaust for the sake of oil and money. After all, the anti-Christ side has a proven track record from World War II.

Presidents Roosevelt and Truman would not even bomb the railroad tracks to the concentration camps, even at the end of the war. At least a million or two million Jews could have been saved. The British did everything in their power to lock the Jews into the Nazi inferno of occupied Europe behind Wehrmacht lines. Since the British and Americans would not let the Jews out, due to Arab oil pressure, Hitler was stuck with them, and so the decision regarding the "Final Solution of the Jewish Problem" was taken. Now, I am not defending Hitler at all. But Hitler was not alone. Churchill and Roosevelt were accomplices. They belonged to the "One World Government."

The inescapable conclusions of that evening on my life were that Christians who love God, the Bible and Israel and the Jewish people must be organized and supported by us so that they, too, can support Israel and a pro-Israel administration in Washington, DC. Otherwise, Washington will be pro-oil, pro-Arab (as it has always been), and will be ready to sacrifice Israel with all its population, five million Jews and Christians plus three million Moslems. It will then "look the other way," while the corporation, big business, petrodollar backed Moslems close in on the kill of the expendable relatively poorer Israel.

It is now the Arabian petrodollar that has Christendom by the jugular. However, since oil reserves are expected to be depleted by seventy years from now and replaced by alternative energy sources, it is the coming decades which will be critical for Islam to impose its will on the world and convert the world to Islam. Or, as Iranian Ayatollah Janati was quoted as saying in Teheran: "The 21st century will be the century of Islam."

The reason for me to write this second book is that it has become clear to me that Christians worldwide will be also sacrificed if necessary for a barrel of oil. The only answer therefore for Israel, America, and the world is a Christian Revival for Israel's Survival.

When I sealed the fifth edition of my first book, in December 1997, it was just days after US Secretary of Defense William Cohen held a live press conference shown on CNN and other TV stations nationwide and worldwide. He held up a five-pound bag of "Domino Sugar" and said: "This much anthrax could destroy the world." He added that "nationalist and religious" terrorists had targeted 28 major US cities for chemical and biological attack. (The allusion was to Saddam Hussein Iraqi state terrorists seeking to reek revenge on the US) It seemed that the showdown with Islam was just around the corner. This appeared at the end of my book. But throughout my book, I had catalogued different Islamic terrorist attacks worldwide including the shooting down of TWA 800, the blowing up of Oklahoma City's Murrah Building, and attacks worldwide on Jews, Christians, Hindus and Buddhists.

So what then happened? Silence. Except for Osama Ben Laden's terrorist attacks on US embassies in Kenya and Tanzania in July 1998 as well as aborted attempts at attacks on other embassies in Kampala, in Uganda, as well as US offices in India. But overall, US civil aviation remained terrorism-free, and major explosions such as the World Trade Center in New York City and Oklahoma City ceased elsewhere in the US. Nor were there biological nor chemical attacks. So what happened? One of the purposes of this, my second book, "Christian Revival for Israel's Survival", is to expose the deal struck between President Clinton, "The Agenda," and the One World Government on the one hand and Islam on the other. This deal with Satan was struck to spare the US economy, so that Wall Street would only go up, up, up. In exchange for this deal with the devil, the enemies of Islam, such as Israel, Serbia, the blacks of Africa, the Christian evangelicals, etc. are to be sacrificed to spare the US economy from instability at best and collapse at worst at the hands of the Islamic agenda. The Clinton Administration and the globalists have now become the defenders of the faith... the Islamic faith and agenda, at the expense of the Jews and Christians.

Again, as I emphasized in my first book, the strategic defense of Israel is my primary concern. While on a cross-country drive in the US in the summer of 1998, a pastor told me about some of his experiences in the US Navy years ago. Considered a candidate for officer training, he was interviewed and asked the following question: "What would you do if ordered to launch a nuclear weapon at the Tel-Aviv (Israeli) coastline?" His answer was: "I am a Christian. I would not envy that ship or any one on board, because should such orders be issued, God Almighty would have that atomic weapon blow up in the hull of that ship." He was immediately dropped from promotion in the officers' course. If the US is so touted as being such an ally of Israel, how could such a question even be considered? As I travel in the US, military and ex-military people approach me and confirm my pulpit message saying that the best officers are being purged from military service because of their patriotism and Christian faith. It turns out that anti-Semites are anti-Christians as well.

Is this policy of anti-Christ Washington DC not a threat to America? Also at risk are the Christians of the world such as the Serbs, whose sovereign lands of 1,300 years are being torn away by the NATO globalist police force in order to be presented as a gift to the Moslem Albanian Kosovars - another sacrifice of Christian interests for the barrel of oil; the two million blacks of southern Sudan genocidally slaughtered by the Islamic government of Khartoum with 6-8 million yet slated for destruction while the world remains silent; 200,000 Christians slaughtered by the Communist government in Beijing; 200,000 dead Catholics on the island of East Timor which was invaded and swallowed up by Indonesia in 1977; Egypt, Pakistan, and many other Islamic countries with their indigenous persecution of all minorities; the Hindus with their endemic Islamic-Pakistani war, the Buddhists, and especially the Chinese with a war brewing in Sinkiang province in the west of China with its Moslems. The list goes on. At risk is anyone who is not a Moslem or not part of the one world government agenda. Ironically, the first to pay for the sins of Islam are the poor Moslems themselves, many of whom disagree with the radical agenda of fanatic Islam but are powerless to act. In fact, Seif Ashmawi, a moderate Moslem, publisher of the Voice of Peace newspaper, was quoted in an article by anti-terrorism expert Steven Emerson in the Wall Street Journal of March 13th, 1996 as saying that moderate Moslems are weakened in the eyes of the Muslim community at large because the White House nurtures its relations with the most radical Moslems. And so, indeed, all of humanity is threatened by the Islamic-globalist agenda.

The purpose of my first book was to warn of the threat to all human beings of fanatic Islam. The purpose of this book is to warn of the surrender of globalism to Islam and the resulting binary Islamic-globalist alliance. May I perhaps suggest possible remedies? foremost among them, repentance, a return to God, or in the case of Bible believing Christians, the only ally the Jews have, Christian Revival for Israel's survival, as well as for that of the world. Another suggested remedy is the debunking and terminating of the Koran, the Hadith and other Islamic texts from which the fanatic Islamic threat is derived and which threatens the Judeo-Christian belief system with its own global Islamic replacement theology.

For America to continue to be the world leader, it must return to being a Judeo-Christian nation as the founding fathers envisioned it. In his book "Democracy in America" Alexis De Toqueville wrote in 1820 that America would become the greatest country in the world because the American people were a good people and their pulpits were "on fire for the Lord." At a White House reception during the Islamic holy month, Ramadan, 1999 for the most radical, fanatic Islamic leaders in the US, President Clinton announced that the US was now a Judeo-Christian-Islamic country. That's like saying: America is now a God-Satan country. America is now a good-evil country. America is now a light-darkness country. For America not to be destroyed as Nineveh and all other great empires in history, it must prove its loyalty exclusively to the God of Abraham, Isaac, and Jacob, the Bible, and the virtues of modern day western civilization and democracy. Islam and Judeo-Christianity cannot be mentioned in the same breath. The Koran is a recipe for "Catch 22" disaster and self-destruction - the overturning of Nineveh, as we look at all the Islamic regimes worldwide. All this is described in "Is Fanatic Islam a Global Threat?"

Again this book does not supercede my first book, but is an extension or continuation of the message with the addition of the natural conclusions reached for America and the world.

Introduction

As in the writing of my first book, I always emphasize my deep belief in the God of Abraham, Isaac and Jacob, in the teachings of the Bible, especially, those teachings confirmed by Jesus of Nazareth in the New Testament: *Love the Lord Thy God, Love Thy Neighbor As Thyself.* ***THESE ARE THE TWO MAIN COMMANDMENTS, THERE ARE NO COMMAND-MENTS GREATER THAN THESE TWO*** (Mark 12:28-31)-(Confirming Deuteronomy 6:49 and Leviticus 19:18). I also emphasize that the Messiah for whom Jews and Christians await will be a Jew who speaks Hebrew. Finally, the basis for all civilization and prosperity comes from God Almighty. Without God, there is nothing. The United States of America was founded on God's principles and God's Bible. The US is being led astray by leaders who are anti-Bible, anti-Israel, and anti-God. This is a threat to Israel, to America and to the world.

President William Jefferson Clinton is purported to have a sign on his desk or somewhere in the Oval Office saying: "It's the economy, stupid." For those of the "Agenda", God, His book the Bible, and the warnings and blessings of the Bible mean nothing except for appearances sake. In fact, President Clinton was quoted in an article by Thomas O'Dwyer on p. A6 of the Israeli English language daily, "The Jerusalem Post" of March 26th, 1999 as saying: "My only enemy is right-wing, religious fundamentalism." Since the most fanatic Islamic fundamentalists are welcome guests in the White House, I suppose this leaves only the Jews and Christians as Clinton's enemies.

Please allow me to quote from Chapter 8 from the Book of Deuteronomy:

1. All the commandment which I command thee this day shall ye observe to do, that ye may live, and mul-

tiply, and go in and possess the land which the Lord swore unto your fathers.

2. And thou shalt remember all the way which the Lord thy God hath led thee these forty years in the wilderness, that He might afflict thee, to prove thee, to know what was in thy heart, whether thou wouldest keep His commandments, or no.

3. And He afflicted thee, and suffered thee to hunger, and fed thee with manna, which thou knewest not neither did thy fathers know; that He might make thee know that man doth not live by bread alone, but by every thing that proceedeth out of the mouth of the Lord doth man live.

4. Thy raiment waxed not old upon thee, neither did thy foot swell, these forty years.

5. And thou shalt consider in thy heart, that, as a man chasteneth his son, so the Lord thy God chasteneth thee.

6. And thou shalt keep the commandments of the Lord thy God, to walk in His ways, and to fear Him.

7. For the Lord thy God bringeth thee into a good land, a land of brooks of water, of fountains and depths, springing forth in valleys and hills.

8. A land of wheat and barley, and vines and fig-trees and pomegranates; a land of olive-trees and honey.

9. A land wherein thou shalt eat bread without scarceness, thou shalt not lack any thing in it; a land whose stones are iron; and out of whose hills thou mayest dig brass.

10. And thou shalt eat and be satisfied, and bless the Lord thy God for the good land which He hath given thee.

11. Beware lest thou forget the Lord thy God, in not keeping His commandments, and His ordinances, and His statutes, which I command thee this day.

12. Lest when thou hast eaten and art satisfied, and hast built goodly houses, and dwelt therein.

13. And; when thy herds and thy flocks multiply, and thy silver and thy gold is multiplied, and all that thou hast is multiplied.

14. Then thy heart be lifted up, and thou forget the Lord thy God, who brought thee forth out of the land of Egypt, out of the house of bondage.

15. Who led thee through the great and dreadful wilderness, wherein were serpents, fiery serpents, and scorpions, and thirsty ground where was no water; who brought thee forth water out of the rock of flint.

16. Who fed thee in the wilderness with manna, which thy fathers knew not; that He might afflict thee, and that He might prove thee, to do thee good at thy latter end.

17. And thou say in thy heart: "My power and the might of my hand hath gotten me this wealth."

18. But thou shalt remember the Lord thy God for it is He that giveth thee power to get wealth; that He may establish His covenant which He swore unto thy fathers, as it is this day.

19. And it shall be, if thou shalt forget the Lord thy God, and walk after other gods, and serve them, and worship them, I forewarn you this day that ye shall surely perish.

20. As the nations that the Lord maketh to perish before you, so shall ye perish; because ye would not hearken unto the voice of the Lord your God.

Though some people would say that the above verses apply only to the Children of Israel during their exodus from Egypt, I would dare to say that the above verses apply equally to America and to the entire world today. When one looks at those countries following the Judeo-Christian ethic, the values of western civilization and democracy, one cannot escape the inspiration that the above verses instill. These are the "haves". In most cases, when one looks at the "have-not" nations of the world, these have not adopted the Judeo-Christian values of western civilization. This is especially true of the Islamic countries, followers of the pagan moon god known as Allah.

In the Islamic teachings, Allah, the moon god, or war god, based on ancient pagan beliefs of Mecca and Medina replaces the God of Abraham, Isaac and Jacob. Before Mohammed's time, there were 360 pagan gods, one for every day of the year. This included the sun, moon, stars, rivers, mountains and rocks. This was sort of a precursor to today's "new-age" beliefs. Mohammed abolished 359 pagan gods leaving the greatest and most fearsome, Allah, the moon-god, as the one monotheistic but still pagan god of Islam. (This is kind of like the ancient pagan Greeks abolishing all the pagan gods except for Zeus as the greatest of all gods. This ancient Greek religion could thus have become monotheistic but still would have remained pagan.)

A reference to the moon-god can be found in Jeremiah 8: 1-3

1. At that time, saith the Lord, they shall bring out the bones of the kings of Judah, and the bones of his princes, and the bones of the priests, and the bones of the prophets, and the bones of the inhabitants of Jerusalem, out of their graves.
2. And they shall spread them before the sun, the moon, and all the host of heaven (the stars), whom they have loved, and whom they have served, and after whom they have walked, and whom they have sought, and whom they have worshipped. They shall not be gathered, nor be buried, they shall be for dung upon the face of the earth.
3. And death shall be chosen rather than life by all of the residue that remain of this evil family, that remain in all the places whither I have driven them, said the Lord of hosts.

This is parallel to what we just saw in Deuteronomy 8: 19.

It is interesting to also look at Jeremiah 9: 22-23:

22: Thus saith the Lord: Let not the wise man glory in his wisdom, Neither let the mighty man glory in his might, Let not the rich man glory in his riches.
23 But let him that glorieth glory in this, that he understandeth and knoweth Me, That I am the Lord

who exercise mercy, justice, and righteousness, in the earth; For in these things I delight, said the Lord.

This is parallel to Deuteronomy 8:17-18:

17. And thou say in thy heart: "My power and the might of my hand hath gotten me this wealth."
18. But thou shalt remember the Lord thy God, for it is He that giveth thee power to get wealth; that He may establish His covenant which He swore unto thy fathers, as it is this day."

Returning to Allah, the moon-god, there is a misconception about the Islamic battle cry "Allahu Akbar!" The translation into English offered by most western media sources is "God is great!" But this is a mistranslation. The word for great in Arabic is kebir. Akbar is diminutive and means either greater or greatest. If it means greater, greater than who? It means greater than the God of Abraham, Isaac and Jacob. In the case of greatest, the meaning is greatest of all pagan gods. But in either case, Allah is not God, the God of Abraham, Isaac and Jacob, but a god, with a small letter g, the moon-god.

According to Islam, the genealogical line is no longer through Isaac and Jacob, but through Ishmael, thus denying the validity of the Bible for Jews and Christians and the divinity of Jesus for Christians (Matthew I). The teachings of love do not appear in the Koran, a book claimed by Moslems to replace the Bible. The word love does not appear even once throughout the Koran! Finally end times eschatology of Islam calls for the annihilation of all Jews, Christians and anyone who is not a Moslem. What would happen to the Messiah who is a Jew and speaks Hebrew on his coming or return is a moot point. This all makes Islam anti-God, anti-Bible, and anti-Messiah or in Christian terminology anti-Christ.

According to Omar M. Ahmad, chairman of a national Islamic watchdog group, "Islam isn't in America to be equal to any other faith, but to become dominant, he said. The Koran, the Muslim book of scripture, should be the highest authority in America, and Islam the only accepted religion on Earth."

"Daily Review" of Hayward, CA, Saturday, July 4th, 1998. Article by Lisa Gardiner.

All this is dealt with in my first book. But like I said, this book is a book of faith based on the Judeo-Christian God of Abraham, Isaac and Jacob, the Bible of this God and the messiah who is a Jew and speaks Hebrew. One who does not believe in these three components may feel aloof to this entire question of the Islamic and now globalist threat. But my contention is that this threat endangers not only the Jews and Christians, but it endangers all people of all faiths (including Moslems). The call to return to God in repentance is a call for all people, including atheists, apostates, and "New-Agers".

The resulting repentance will save the world from calamity. The alternative is the victory of the Islamic-globalist alliance which I believe will, God-forbid, destroy or overturn the world as was prophesied by Jonah in the city of Nineveh. Thanks to the repentance of Nineveh, at that time, the city was spared in that generation.

My belief is that if we remain loyal to the tenets of the Bible, to the God of Abraham, Isaac and Jacob, and truly seek repentance and God's direction, Israel, America and the world will be spared. My prayer is that this book will contribute to that goal. It can only happen through God's word, the Bible.

Chapter One

The Rise and Fall of American Jewry

In trying to understand what makes the one world government agenda increasingly merge with the Islamic agenda, it is necessary to analyze demographics: the decrease in the number of Jews and increase in the number of Moslems in America and worldwide. This is the first stage in America distancing itself from the God of Abraham, Isaac and Jacob.

From the very first day of colonization at Plymouth Rock in 1620, the first pilgrims coming to America sought to establish a godly community that would serve the Lord and farm the land. These Christian pilgrims were also fleeing persecution from the mainline Anglican Church of England. Later groups arriving in America included Puritans, Huguenots, Mennonites, Amish, and others, all fleeing the persecution of mainline churches in their home countries. All these people wanted was religious freedom to serve the Lord as best as they saw fit and to be able to farm the land - to build, and to be built up.

When the first Jews arrived in the Americas fleeing the persecution of the Catholic, Lutheran and Orthodox churches, they were received as basically just another "church" group. Later, when the mainline churches arrived in the new colonies, they, too, were just considered another "church" group, instead of "the Church."

America from its very inception was a patchwork of many ethnic groups and diverse religious communities. The Jews were never ever persecuted, tortured or killed in America because of their Judaism. On the contrary, they were only blessed. As it says in the Bible: Those who bless Israel are blessed, and those who curse Israel are cursed. (Genesis 27:29 & and Numbers

24:9) I think this is the main reason that God blessed America and made it world power #1. Let's pray it remains that way.

Whereas in most Christian and Islamic countries Jews were never able to fully participate in the life of the nation collectively, in America, they were blessed and allowed to become active in almost all spheres of American life. This includes government, the military, academe, commerce, agriculture, and even space exploration just to mention a few.

But here is the catch. Too much of a blessing becomes a curse. I can remember as a young man growing up in America, that our population reached about six million American Jews. We were number three after the Catholics and Protestants. There were virtually no Muslims, Hindus, Buddhists, or adherents of other religions.

But today as we are about to enter the 21st century, the Jews take a poor fourth place in America after the Muslims, who, according to CNN, total over 14 million people in the US. According to statistics in my possession, the Jews number about 4.5 million Jews in the US.

When I made "aliyah," or moved to Israel in 1968, I never lost touch with the realities of Jewish demography back in the States. Starting from 1970, there was considerable immigration, though low- key from the Soviet Union of Jews who preferred not to move to Israel. Some estimates put the numbers at about one million. In addition, the phenomenon of "yordim" or those who have lived in Israel and "going down" from Israel to America also reached anywhere between half a million to one million from 1948. I know from my own family and connections in Argentina that about a quarter of million Jews from Argentina moved to the US in the last 30 years as well. Without being too much of a mathematical wizard, one can see how, together with natural reproduction, the Jews should have reached about ten million in the US. Yet, our numbers hover around the 4.5 million-mark. So where are between 5 and 6 million Jews hiding?

The answer is twofold: assimilation and the failure to reproduce. A myriad of books has been written about the question of Jewish assimilation throughout history. It is not the purpose of this book to go into the subject of assimilation. It is common knowledge that over the last three thousand years the Jewish people should have been as numerous as the Chinese, or the Hindus. But due to dispersion, persecution and assimilation the Jews have disappeared as a distinct national, ethnic or religious group, though their genes are to be found virtually in every country of the world.

But a problem even more insidious is the Jewish failure to procreate and propagate our people in America. Too much of a blessing has become a curse. As the Jews prospered and became able to pay (with tremendous loans and mortgages) for their children's college and post-graduate education, one, and perhaps even two generations of reproduction were skipped. For decades young Jewish men and women have chosen to live like priests in order to attain an academic title or degree. Success means everything. They marry later, usually marry out of the faith, and finally, the biological clock has ticked so much so that in the "best case scenario" one child becomes the limit.

When I was a young man, I had the privilege of corresponding with Israel's first Prime Minister, David Ben Gurion. In one of his letters to me, he prophesied that Israel had to double from 3 million to 6 million or even triple its population to 9 million in order to survive. As for the Jews of the Diaspora, Ben Gurion said they were doomed to assimilate and disappear. How true his prophecy was. Israel in 1999 is now close to 5 million Jews, while the American Jewish community is disappearing.

At the present rate, in another thirty years, the Jewish population in America, I believe, will shrink to less than 3 million Jews. Another problem in the Jewish community is that roughly 80% of America's Jews have never visited Israel, are not active in Jewish organizations or philanthropy, and have never read the Bible. I call these Jews "Jews for nothing." They just don't care about Judaism, God or the Bible.

I am often criticized in certain Jewish communities for visiting and sharing with "messianic" groups. In most cases, the overwhelming majority of the members of these groups are not Jewish at all, but simply Christians seeking their Jewish roots and a more Judaic content to their Christianity. In cases where there are Jews who have become Christians in these groups, their commitment to Israel, the Bible, and the God of Abraham,

Isaac and Jacob has only increased. "But the 'messianics' are our worst enemy," my critics say. "No," I reply, "we are our own worst enemy." The "messianics" cannot be blamed for the disappearance in America of five million Jews in 30 years. This failure to reproduce and to be committed to the survival of the Jewish people is the worst enemy. The "messianics" love the God of Abraham, Isaac and Jacob, love the Bible, love Israel, and as such are allies just as the Bible-believing Christians are. They are to be encouraged and mobilized in the battle for the survival of Israel.

Here comes the bad news. The Islamic world has always viewed the US as the guarantor of the survival of Israel. The US was always perceived as the puppeteer and Israel the puppet. Without the US, Israel would not be able to exist. So a strategic decision was taken, I believe, in the 1980's in the Arab and Islamic countries to drive a wedge into America that eventually would cause the US to distance itself from Israel and eventually, even turn on Israel, God-forbid.

The first stage in this process was simply buying out the leadership of America with oil and the petrodollar. This was dealt with in my first book "Is Fanatic Islam a Global Threat?" This problem actually predates World War II. The Arabs had the oil in the 1920's, 30's, and 40's and threatened the British and Americans that they would go over to Hitler's side if the Jews were allowed to emigrate from Europe to Palestine, to England, to the US or anywhere else in the world for that matter. The Jews' destiny was to be incinerated in the concentration camps, and the Arabs had their way. And nothing has changed since 1945.

What has changed is the mass immigration to the US of Islamic students and later their families from Islamic countries. Within two decades, the Moslems have reached about 15 million people in America. The universities have been financially bribed or "encouraged" to open their gates to Islamic students. This is a process with long term goals. If this process continues, within another two decades there will be about 30 million Moslems in America, roughly ten times the Jewish population, and perhaps even larger than the population of the "born-again" evangelical, Bible Christians who love Israel. What does that say tactically and strategically for Israel? The writing is on the wall.

I have recently begun working closely with a very special group in the US: Aglow International. This is a Christian organization numbering close to half a million women throughout the world. According to information they have provided me, assimilation is no longer an exclusively Jewish problem. At least 10,000 American children born to Christian mothers and Moslem fathers have been illegally abducted to the Middle East by their fathers. The US State Department and other official agencies cannot or will not do anything to restore these children to their mothers for obvious reasons.

Over the last two decades, millions of Moslem men have come to study in the US, and marry Christian women, which is permissible under Islamic law. In some cases they take their brides back to the Islamic lands where the latter lose all the rights they were accustomed to back home. Examples of this marriage brokering system are detailed in my first book. These men are allowed by Islamic law to marry an additional one, two or three wives without even consulting with their first Christian wife. Some times, they arrive in the US already married to one wife or more before marrying their American Christian wife. They conveniently forget to tell the naive, believing American woman that they already have a wife or even more than one wife "back home."

The offspring of these marriages by Islamic law in Islamic lands must be Moslems. The Christian wife has no say in the matter. If she disagrees, he can simply divorce her or as it says in Chapter 4 verse 34 of the Koran: "Men have authority over women because Allah has made the one superior to the other, and because they spend their wealth to maintain them. Good women are obedient. They guard their unseen parts because Allah has guarded them. As for those from whom you fear disobedience, admonish them and send them to beds apart and beat them."

Many Christian women have accompanied their Moslem spouses back to the Middle East never to be seen or heard of again. Many Christians have come up to me in the 300 churches I have spoken in and have asked for my help in tracking down their daughters and sisters in Islamic lands. Moslem men go by different laws. They go by a different book, the Koran. They go by a different god, Allah.

But strategically, there is no doubt that these Moslem men who have come into the US and Canada in recent years are part of an overall plan to change the demographics from being pro-Judeo-Christian, to demographics which increasingly turn away from and eventually turn against Judeo-Christianity.

Islamic leaders from all over the world have invested billions of dollars in the establishment of Islamic chairs, and Islamic studies departments in American universities. University officials always seeking new sources of funds for university coffers eagerly responded. The result is that the floodgates have been opened, and the US has received an Islamic population of 15 million in the last few decades. Strategically for the Islamic world, this has been a brilliant move and will be continued until America is pried away from Israel and Judeo-Christianity and becomes increasingly subservient to the agenda of the Islamic petrodollar.

Whatever the outcome though, the attractiveness and power of the Jewish community in the US is on the wane, while that of Islam is growing frenetically. This is not lost on President Clinton, as well as any president succeeding him. In fact, during the 1992 presidential election campaign which President George Bush lost, former Secretary of State James Baker III once used a four-letter expletive to describe his attitude toward American Jews and said, "They're only four million and they don't vote for us anyway." Many people said to me, "President George Bush withheld the $10 billion in loan guarantees for Israel when it was being deluged with a million Russian immigrants and needed these loans, so God ended his term of office." Judgement is God's alone.

It will be interesting to see God's judgement of President William Jefferson Clinton, who brought brutal pressure to bear on Israel's Prime Minister Benjamin Netanyahu between 1996-1999. It will be even more interesting to see how Prime Minister Ehud Barak will manage with President Clinton's arm twisting or rather arm-breaking.

Finally, I would like to conclude this chapter on the decline of American Jewry with an article by James Dao from the The New York Times Sunday February 28th, 1999 as it appeared the following day in The Jerusalem Post Israeli English language daily:

"Hillary Rodham Clinton said last year that a Palestinian state was "very important" to Middle East peace, and it seemed like a monumental political gaffe. Many Jewish groups reacted with alarm. And her husband's Administration, which has never endorsed the idea, swiftly disowned her comments.

Now, after 10 months, Mrs. Clinton's words are back on the front pages of New York City's Jewish newspapers, thanks to the First Lady's announcement that she is thinking about running for the Senate from the Empire State next year.

One of her potential Republican rivals, Mayor Rudolph W. Giuliani, has stoked the controversy, asserting that Mrs. Clinton's remarks were "a very big mistake." And analysts are already predicting that the First Lady's position on Palestinian statehood will hurt her among Jewish voters, about 12 percent of the state's electorate.

But it's not necessarily so. A Palestinian state is not the same hot-button issue it was 10, or even 5 years ago, when endorsing the concept was akin in some peoples' minds to endorsing terrorism, many political analysts and Jewish leaders say.

'The Palestinian state is no longer the taboo subject it once was,' said Thomas Smerling, Washington director of the Israel Policy Forum, an American Jewish group that supports the peace process. 'At a time when you have a Likud Prime Minister negotiating with the Chairman of the PLO over the size of an eventual Palestinian entity, the idea of a Palestinian state no longer seems as alarming as it once did.'

Many Jewish leaders say that since Israel and the Palestine Liberation Organization recognized each other's legitimacy in 1993, a growing number of Jews in America and Israel have come to accept that some sort of Palestinian state will be the likely outcome of a negotiated peace process.

Several polls of American Jews conducted over the past three years support that notion. A 1998 poll commissioned by the Middle East Quarterly found that 64% of American Jews

supported the statement, 'The Palestinians should have their
own country.'

But even if most American Jews believe a Palestinian state
is desirable, or inevitable, Mrs. Clinton's statement could still
cause her grief in a New York campaign. Many Jews were
troubled not so much by the wording of Mrs. Clinton's remarks
as by their timing. From Washington, she spoke up in the middle
of sensitive peace talks between Israel and Palestinians. To
many, weighing in at that moment seemed a crass attempt to
push the talks toward a conclusion favoring the Palestinians.

'Many Jews viewed her statement as supporting a unilat-
eral declaration of statehood by the Palestinians, or at least
granting Arafat a license to do it,' said Abraham Foxman, national director of the Anti-Defamanation League of B'nai B'rith,
referring to Yasir Arafat, the Palestinian leader.

But Mr. Foxman also acknowledges that 'the overwhelming number of Jews would be supportive' of a Palestinian state
if it were the result of a negotiated settlement. 'It's Israel's peace,'
he said.

In a sign that she is serious about becoming a candidate,
Mrs. Clinton has been trying to repair any damage from her
remarks. Meeting with rabbis last week in Washington, she said
she supported both the peace process and a Palestinian state.
'They are not mutually exclusive of one another,' her spokeswoman, Marsha Berry, said.

After the meeting, Rabbi Jay Kornsgold of New Jersey told
the newspaper Jewish Week, 'This may impress a lot of Jews in
New York.'

If supporting a Palestinian state is no longer the third rail
of Jewish-American politics, what might Mr. Giuliani or other
Republican gain from keeping the issue alive?

A significant number of Jews continue to oppose a Palestinian state. But they tend to be conservatives who vote Republican anyway. It is more likely that Mr. Giuliani was using the
Palestinian issue as a symbol for broader themes, political analysts said.

Raising questions about Mrs. Clinton's remarks is a way
of raising doubts about her support for Israel, said Kieran
Mahoney, a Republican consultant from New York. It also is

another way of labeling her a liberal ideologue, said Ester Fuchs, a political science professor at Barnard College.

'Supporting a Palestinian state used to be a peacenik position, an extreme left-wing position,' she said. 'And that's what Giuliani has to do: Paint his opponent into a left-wing corner.'

Mr. Giuliani says he has simply taken the same position as the President, who is very popular among Jews. But in helping to keep the issue alive, he risks a backlash, some analysts contend. Last year, Senator Alfonse M. D'Amato accused Charles E. Schumer, who is Jewish, of missing votes on important Jewish issues. Mr. D'Amato lost the race and saw his share of the Jewish vote decline from past elections.

'I'm not sure the Mayor has the pulse of American Jewish opinion on this issue,' said Seymour D. Reich, a past chairman of the Conference of Presidents of Major American Jewish Organizations and a supporter of the peace process."

All the above are warning signals of a growing strategic threat facing the State of Israel from within the US: The complacent, shrinking Jewish population and Hillary Clinton, merely another player in the globalist agenda. The only friends of Israel that can and must stand in the gap for Israel are the born-again, evangelical Christians. You are not our best friends. You are our only friends. You truly understand the existential threat to Israel from the creation, God-forbid, of a Palestinian-Islamic state in the Holy Land. This is why there must be a Christian revival for Israel's survival. The more people who join this revival, the more allies Israel will have. The better will be its chances for survival.

I will conclude this first chapter with excerpts from a small disturbing article by Jim Irwin that appeared in the Jerusalem Post of Thursday, June 24th, 1999.

Amr Moussa:
Mideast Gains From Arab-American Clout

Dearborn, Michigan (AP) - The Middle East stands to benefit from Arab-Americans' growing economic and political clout in this country, Egyptian Foreign Minister Amr Moussa said.

Moussa told a mostly Arab-American audience Tuesday that Egypt's strides toward a market economy have made it an attractive place for foreign investment.

He appealed specifically to business interests in southeast Michigan - "the heartland of Arab America" - to take advantage of Egypt's growing infrastructure, liberalized trade agreements and promotion of private investment.

"The legacy of public sector domination of the economy is over," he said, adding that other Middle Eastern nations are following Egypt's lead.

But Moussa said closer economic ties between the US and the Arab world should be independent of the still-touchy relations between the Arab countries and Israel.

The Detroit area, home to 250,000 to 300,000 people of Arab descent, was one of four stops on Moussa's visit to the US. In Dearborn, he visited the offices of the Arab Community Center for Economic and Social Services, one of the nation's largest Arab social service agencies, and received a key to the city from Mayor Michael Guido.

"I really feel at home in this city," Moussa said.

Chapter Two

"It's the economy, stupid!"

It happened during my travels in the US on Tuesday, April 20th, 1999. Two high school seniors, part of a group called the "Trench Coat Mafia," walked into Columbine High School in Littleton, Colorado, and snuffed out the lives of 13 students and one faculty member with various weapons and bombs. Another 20 were critically wounded.

There were voices of rage and protest. Many blamed the parents for the deeds of the children. None of this would have happened, had the parents been good parents. It later turned out that the parents, if not exemplary parents, were really not responsible for the sins of their children. Then, another scapegoat was sought: The National Rifle Association and those who own guns. Talk show celebrity Rosie O'Donnell said all gun owners should be jailed because without guns, these teenagers would never have committed their atrocities. Of course, President Clinton attacked the NRA and has been trying to pass new gun control laws, the final purpose being the annulling of Amendment 2 of the US Constitution. Finally, President Clinton backtracked and said to the NRA: "Let's work together."

But what is the root cause of the malaise that caused these two young men to take the lives of others, and then to take their own lives? As I wrote in the Preface, Introduction, and 1st chapter of this book, there is a system. It is called the system of the God of Abraham, Isaac, and Jacob. This system is duly encoded in a book known as the Bible. It is a system that succeeds. Straying from the system leads to self-destruction. It has been there available for us for almost 3,500 years. It is what made America great. Judeo-Christian democracy and western civilization are its fruits.

One of the most famous sections of this system is known as the "10 Commandments". Please consider a few of these commandments. Thou shalt not lie. Thou shalt not commit adultery. Thou shalt steal. Thou shalt not murder. Thou shalt not covet thy neighbor's wife and possessions. Thou shalt not bear false witness against thy neighbor.

When a president of the US has an approval rating of 70% in spite of violating all or some of the above, because, after all, "It is the economy, stupid," then that is a statement about the people of America. When actress Barbara Streisand is quoted as saying: "Hey, we didn't vote for the Pope," she was de-legitimizing morality. When the only criteria for the success of the president is keeping Wall Street above 10,000 and keeping the US economy on an even keel, this sends a message. When the President, who is a role model, perhaps the role model for the US, can get away with virtually anything, so what's wrong with shooting up a school? What's wrong with doing anything wrong? There is a system. When the leader strays from the system, so will the youth. This is my conclusion drawn from the Columbine school incident.

Another conclusion drawn from this tragic incident stems from the fixation of American youth, as well as Americans of all ages with the computer. In the case of Dylan Klebold and Eric Harris, they even had an Internet web site espousing hate and bigotry besides promoting anarchy. They were addicts of virtual reality bloody and violent computer games.

On the one hand, watching violent TV programs, video movies or playing violent virtual reality computer games is eventually going to "program" people into violence in real life. Similarly, as Wall Street reached new heights in 1999, so, too, are normally productive people mesmerized and turned into non-productive zombies as they watch the Las Vegas email casino known as e-trade.

Wall Street and the computer have turned from being vital economic tools of world growth, into vices enslaving people globally. The bottom line is that God has become ignored - a burdensome stone. His word is disregarded, and self-destruction, I believe, is inevitable. But, again, only God is the judge of us all. Maybe the Y2K computer bug is a reminder of who really is in control.

If President Clinton's motto is: "It's the economy, stupid," I think a new sign should be hanging over the Oval Office saying, "No stupid. It's not the economy. It is God." Pray for President Clinton. He needs to repent. He needs to be part of the Christian revival for Israel's Survival.

In my first book, I quote the twelfth chapter of the New Testament's Book of Revelation regarding the beast and the moon underneath the feet of the woman bearing the child. The pastor, whom I listened to preaching in the church in Beaumont, Texas, interpreted the beast as Islam, the mother Israel, and the child the Christian world.

In my most recent visit to the US, another Christian interpreted the first verses of Chapter 17 regarding the whore riding the beast.

1. And there came one of the seven angels which had the seven vials, and talked with me, saying unto me, Come hither; I will show unto thee the judgement of the great whore that sitteth upon many waters:
2. With whom the kings of the earth have committed fornication, and the inhabitants of the earth have been made drunk with the wine of her fornication.
3. So he carried me away in the spirit into the wilderness: and I saw a woman sit upon a scarlet colored beast, full of names of blasphemy, having seven heads and ten horns.
4. And the woman was arrayed in purple and scarlet color, and decked with gold and precious stones and pearls, having a golden cup in her hand full of abominations and filthiness of her fornication;
5. And upon her forehead was a name written, MYSTERY, BABYLON THE GREAT, THE MOTHER OF HARLOT'S AND ABOMINATIONS OF THE EARTH.
6. And I saw the woman drunken with the blood of the saints and with the blood of the martyrs of Jesus:

and when I saw her, I wondered with great admiration.

A possible interpretation of these verses is as follows: The whore is the "globalist one world government." The beast is mammon-rich Islam paying the whore for her services. The blood of the saints is that of the Jews. The blood of the martyrs of Jesus is that of the Christians.

Chapter Three

"What ever happened to Saddam Hussein?"

On Thursday, May 27, 1999, President Slobodan Milosevic of Yugoslavia was indicted by the UN War Crimes Tribunal in the city of Hague, the Netherlands. He is being blamed for the deaths of 10,000 Albanian Kosovars and the expulsion of hundreds of thousands from Kosovo to Albania, Macedonia, and other countries.

At the very end of my first book "Is Fanatic Islam a Global Threat?" I painted a gloomy picture of state terrorism by Iraq and its elusive survivor of a leader Saddam Hussein. Saddam Hussein, commonly nicknamed the "Butcher of Baghdad," is responsible for being the Iraqi reincarnation of Adolf Hitler. Of course, the first to suffer from his rule, have been his very own Iraqi people. Millions of his citizens have died directly or indirectly from his very rule.

Saddam Hussein is responsible for starting a war with Iran in 1980. This lasted until 1988 and exacted a human toll on both sides topping one million innocent dead Moslems. He later invaded Kuwait exacting the deaths of hundreds of thousands more people in addition to the expelling or flight of one million Egyptians back to Egypt, hundreds of thousands of Palestinians scattered all over the world and basically the rape, theft and destruction of Kuwait. When he was defeated in Desert Storm, he set alight the Kuwaiti oilfields out of spite causing immeasurable ecological damage still being felt today. Saddam Hussein even used poison gas and chemicals to kill 8,000 of his own Iraqi people in the town of Khalabja in Kurdistan.

After his defeat, Saddam Hussein blamed the US and UN for economic sanctions, which, he claimed took another two million lives of innocent women, children and the elderly. The reply of the US and UN was "Replace Saddam Hussein with another leader, and the sanctions will be removed." As a result of the failure to dislodge Saddam Hussein, the sanctions have been in place until today.

In February 1993, the World Trade Center, in New York City, was bombed by Islamic fundamentalist terrorists in league with Saddam Hussein. It has been proved beyond a doubt by researcher Dr. Laurie Mylroie that this was a Saddam Hussein, Iraqi "state" terrorism bomb aimed at toppling the Twin Trade Towers that would have caused anywhere between 20,000 to 200,000 dead had the bombing succeeded. I also show how the terrorist car bombing of the Murrah Federal Building in Oklahoma City was an Islamic-Iraqi bombing. So, too, was TWA-800 brought down by a missile, probably an Islamic missile of Soviet manufacture. The purpose of this "state" terrorism was to reek revenge on America for what it had done to Iraq.

In my first book I document how Saddam Hussein has built up his network of hit teams and terrorist squads in the US ready at a moment's notice to cause Wall Street to crash, followed by the entire US economy. Again, as I said in the Preface of this book, all of a sudden, something happened. America had been in "check mate" at the hands of the Islamic terrorist agenda, but then all became "quiet on the western front." The Dow Jones Index of Wall Street climbed to 10,000 and even to 11,000.

In my first book, I pleaded for the world to show mercy on the Iraqi people, as well as to show leadership in ridding the world of this menace, Saddam Hussein. I called on the UN to remove Saddam from power, not to kill him - merely to incarcerate him until free elections were held in Iraq. The UN should impose a civilian administration over all of Iraq, much as it did in occupied western Germany at the end of the WWII. The ideal solution would be the rebuilding of Iraq under now democratic circumstances under the aegis of the UN, the freeing of the Iraqi people from under the unbearable yolk of Saddam Hussein, and basically the creation of the first democratic Arab state of its kind in the world.

Of course, none of this ever happened. It seems it was in someone's interest to keep Saddam Hussein in power. He could have been "taken out" by "stormin" Norman Schwartzkopf, at the head of allied troops in March 1991. I described in my book how President Clinton similarly botched three attempts at removing Saddam Husssein during his terms of office.

In January 1999, I arrived in the US at the beginning of a new cross-country journey in my van starting with a drive south to Florida. When I arrived in Georgia, I found the price of the gallon of unleaded gas at 67 cents! This was the lowest price since 1973 and the Arab oil embargo following the Israeli-Arab Yom Kippur War. The price of the barrel of oil on the international markets had sunk to a low of $9.00 a barrel, also the lowest it had been in decades.

Then, all of a sudden, the prices quickly went up, really rather artificially, at the behest of the OPEC oil countries and the oil companies. The price of the barrel of oil had to go back up to $18 for the oil companies to make a profit, so they claimed. One thing was sure, sanctions were not to be lifted on Iraqi oil exports, because that would make the oil prices drop to $6.00 a barrel. So, the Iraqi people were to continue to be saddled with one of the most ruthless, terrorist, despotic rulers in the world because that way, sanctions did not have to be lifted.

My heart cries out for the Iraqi people. Our forefathers, Abraham, Isaac, and Jacob were ancient "Iraqis". It became evident to me that even though the Iraqis are predominantly Moslems, they too would be sacrificed for OPEC's barrel of oil. Saddam Hussein really is guilty for the deaths of millions of his own people as well as that of his neighbors. He really is guilty for an unprovoked attack on Israel with 39 scuds, guilty of terrible ecological damage, and finally guilty of international terrorism that could have caused and may yet cause the deaths of millions. Yet he is not being brought before the international tribunal in Hague, Netherlands. Slobodan Milosevic, who has been witness to the methodic stripping down of Serbia of its lands by the "one world government agenda" can always claim the backing and loyalty of the Serbian people for trying to defend Yugoslav sovereignty. Ethnic cleansing is terrible, and all sides of the conflict in the Balkans are guilty of that. Whatever crimes Milosevic may be guilty of pale in comparison to the crimes of war criminal Saddam Hussein.

The nagging question always recurs: Why did Presidents Bush and Clinton not finish the job with Saddam with the millions of people he has killed and still ruthlessly rules?

The following are newspaper articles taken from the New York Times and Jerusalem Post English language daily of Israel. They may be considered as a continuation of other articles that appeared in my first book "Is Fanatic Islam a Global Threat?"

Germs, Atoms and Poison Gas: The Iraqi Shell Game

The New York Times, Sunday Edition of December 20th, 1998. Article by William J. Broad and Judith Miller.

Sometimes past is prologue. As Iraqi officials in 1995 led United Nations arms inspectors to a large cache of documents hidden on a chicken farm near Baghdad, a red photograph album stood out. At first glance, the album, like the half million pages of other papers in the shed, seemed to cast light on Iraq's secret drive to obtain germ, chemical and nuclear arms and missiles.

But closer scrutiny revealed huge gaps. The album's dozens of pages, for instance, offered some insights into Iraq's germ efforts. Photo after captioned photo showed not only flasks of deadly agents like anthrax but animal test subjects small and large, including sheep.

Yet the inspectors found that the album covered germ work only through 1989 - before Baghdad embarked on a crash program to turn experimentation into weapons for the 1991 gulf war, in which it deployed germ bombs and warheads at four sites, but did not use them.

Moreover, something else was missing. The numbered pages were interrupted where photos had been removed from the three-ring binder.

"We don't know what was taken," one inspector said. "My guess? Pictures showing people" central to building the arsenal.

Today, seven years after President Saddam Hussein promised to come clean about his weapons of mass destruction, the book on Iraqi arms is still full of holes.

Military experts in Washington and at the UN say the unanswered questions are serious and legion. Still unaccounted for are hundreds of chemical arms, tons of nerve gas, more than 100 germ weapons and parts for up to four nuclear warheads, which are said to lack only the uranium to fuel them.

"There are vast areas of activity that are still unknown to us," said Gary Milhollin, director of the Wisconsin Project on Nuclear Arms Control in Washington and an expert on Iraq's arsenal. "The uncertainties are so great that, as far as we know, Saddam Hussein today could have both chemical and germ warfare agents in warheads, ready to go."

Mr. Milhollin and his staff have prepared a list of some of the main riddles about Iraq's unconventional weapons. Their chart is lengthy. Yet Mr. Milhollin and UN experts note that no such list can be exhaustive. Given Iraq's evasiveness and defiance, its stonewalling and lies, such listings can only suggest the depth of the remaining questions.

"This is not definitive," one inspector said of the chart, adding that the goal was out of reach even of the UN and Federal intelligence agencies.

Prospects for greater illumination are bleak, analysts say, because of both the unknown consequences of the bombing that began Wednesday and Baghdad's obstinacy. What evidence might have been destroyed in the bombing was unknowable, but the inspection process, most analysts agree, had all but collapsed.

Richard Butler, chairman of the UN Special Commission (UNSCOM) in charge of arms inspectors in Iraq, is more diplomatic. "It must regrettably be recorded again," he told the Security Council on Tuesday, "that the commission is not able to conduct the substantive disarmament work mandated to it."

The stakes are potentially huge. Iraq has already confessed to having made enough deadly microbes to kill all the people on Earth several times over. And Saddam Hussein has used weapons of mass destruction before.

After losing the 1991 gulf war, Mr. Hussein, as a condition of surrender, agreed to declare within 15 days all his nuclear, chemical and biological arms and the missiles for delivering them, and then to destroy them.

The UN set up a group to insure that he kept his word. Until it verified destruction of the weapons, Iraq was barred from selling oil. Later the UN relented a bit and allowed some oil exports to pay for food, medicine and war reparations.

To date, those sanctions have cost Iraq more than $120 billion. Eager to escape them, Baghdad over the years has offered at least five different "full, final and complete" disclosures, but the UN officials have dismissed these as woefully incomplete.

An example of Iraq's pale cooperation is demonstrated in the 1995 chicken farm haul, which was one of the special commission's greatest finds. While the documents were valuable, they had been carefully culled and included nothing from the headquarters of the Military Industrialization Corporation or the relevant archives of the Ministry of Defense.

Among the ugliest outstanding questions is whether Iraq tested its germ weapons on people. Rumors and even some suggestive photographs have come to light. But so far, there is neither proof nor admissions.

Recently, the battle for truth about Iraq's armaments has been crippled by diminishing returns.

The latest round of inspections aimed at testing Iraq's compliance with UN resolutions was an abject failure. In interviews, inspectors told of astonishing Iraqi feints and what one non-American inspector called a saga of "lies and deception."

"UN Inspectors: Saddam still has biological weapons"

Article by Douglas Davis in the Jerusalem Post of Monday, December 21, 1998.

"Iraqi President Saddam Hussein is continuing to hide stocks of biological weapons and delivery systems, according to UN weapons inspectors.

Senior British inspector David Kelly reported that Iraqi officials stymied attempts by the inspectors to find documents which would have led them to the concealed weapons.

These weapons, he said, were particularly dangerous because they were small, could be easily hidden and regenerated.

Before the 1990 invasion of Kuwait, it is known that iraq had 6,000 liters of anthrax, 8,425 liters of botulinum toxin, 2,200 liters of aflatoxin (which cuases liver cancer) and a quantity of clostridium perfringens (which causes gangrene.)

Only a small quantity of these agents was subsequently discovered.

In addition, Iraq had built 157 aerial bombs, 50 of which were armed with anthrax, and again, only a few have been discovered.

According to the London "Sunday Times," 'more than 30,000 munitions filled with chemical weapons and 4,000 tons of precursor chemicals, which Iraq claims to have destroyed, are still unaccounted for.'

It also has several tons of VX nerve agent, as well as sarin and mustard gas.

Iraq is also believed to have 'a few' Scud missiles and four mobile Scud launchers.

A confidential report sent to New York by the weapons inspectors just before last week's air strikes noted that Iraq still has equipment that would allow it to restart its nuclear program.

The report stated that unless Saddam was stripped of biological weapons and the means to produce them, he could assemble a new arsenal in a matter of months.

Former leader of the arms inspection team Scott Ritter, writing in the London 'Mail on Sunday' doubted that the air strikes had made a serious impact on Iraq's non-conventional weapons stockpile.

When he took over as leader of the inspection team, he said, Saddam was "stockpiling components for long-range ballistic missiles that could hit Israel."

He had also amassed "cookbooks" that contain the processes to make chemical and biological agents that could kill hundreds of thousands of people.

"If you want to calculate the chances of a short bombing campaign getting rid of his weapons potential," said Ritter, "remember that one delivery van could hold enough gas to wipe out a city. Then imagine trying to locate it in just three days."

He added: "Saddam will still have his arsenal and he will be able to portray himself as the little guy who stood up to the Great Satan."

"IRAQ THREATENS TO ATTACK US BASES IN TURKEY AND GULF"

Article by Leon Barkho in the Jerusalem Post of Tuesday, February 16, 1999.

Baghdad (AP) - Iraq will attack Incirlik, the US base in southeastern Turkey, if its planes continue to overfly northern Iraq, Vice President Taha Yassin Ramadan warned yesterday.

It was the first time Iraq has threatened to attack Turkey in many years.

In an interview with Radio Monte Carlo, monitored in Baghdad, Ramadan said Iraq is going to attack the US and British bases in neighboring states, because their planes are patrolling the "no-fly" zones over northern and southern Iraq.

He said the warning applies to Incirlik and bases in Saudi Arabia and Kuwait.

"If the Turkish base continued attacking Iraq it will certainly be targeted like the other bases," Ramadan said.

Ramadan made his remarks the same day that Iraqi Deputy Prime Minister Tariq Aziz held talks with Turkish Prime Minister Bulent Ecevit in Ankara. Aziz came to Turkey to try to persuade the Turkish government to put a halt to the overflights from Incirlik.

But Ecevit made it clear that US planes would continue to maintain the no-fly zone from Incirlik. He told reporters he had told Aziz the mission is operating under strict Turkish control and that US jets are striking Iraqi defense sites only when attacked or targeted.

Ramadan reiterated the threat made Sunday, after a meeting of the leadership chaired by President Saddam Hussein, that Iraq would attack the US bases and British bases in Kuwait and Saudi Arabia, whose places patrol the no-fly zone over southern Iraq.

"I say if America and Britain do not retreat, they'll soon pay dearly in relation to the properties and elements they use to launch aggression on the people of Iraq," Ramadan said.

In Kuwait yesterday, a Foreign Ministry spokesman said the Iraqi leadership's statement showed Baghdad's "aggressive intention toward its neighbors."

Iraq's warning Sunday was a "direct and serious threat to Kuwait's security and sovereignty," the spokesman told the official Kuwait News Agency.

The Arab League yesterday dismissed Iraq's threats against Kuwait and Saudi Arabia as unacceptable.

"We do not accept threats," Secretary-General Esmat Abdel Meguid told reporters after talks with the Kuwaiti leadership. "Problems are not solved by threats. They are solved through dialogue and negotiations."

The Iraqi warning said Saudi Arabia and Kuwait should distance themselves from the US and Britain. It did not specify what type of action Baghdad would take against the bases.

The no-fly zones were set up after the 1991 Gulf War to prevent Iraqi aircraft from attacking rebels in the north and south of the country.

Iraq has never accepted the validity of the zones, which were created by the US, Britain, and France and are not authorized by a specific UN Security Council resolution. France later withdrew its participation in the enforcement of the zones.

Also yesterday, US warplanes attacked defense sites in northern Iraq, the Defense Department said in Washington.

SADDAM CALLS ON IRAQIS TO PREPARE TO BATTLE US

Article from AP appearing in The Jerusalem Post of Monday, June 14th, 1999.

President Saddam Hussein has urged Iraqis to start military training and be ready to combat the American "enemy," the official media reported yesterday.

Addressing his top military commanders, Saddam also scoffed at his Arab neighbors for providing US troops with military bases and facilities.

"We have no other option but to train the men and to continue training," Saddam was quoted by the ruling Baath Party newspaper "Al-Thawra." "This is not only to prepare people for combat to defend their country, but also to give them impetus to face difficulties."

"Al-Thawra" said Saddam predicted that the Americans will be defeated in the event of a confrontration with Iraq.

"We are nearing the day in which the enemy will announce by itself that it has no alternative but to leave" the region, Saddam said.

Saddam said without help from some of Iraq's Arab neighbors, the US could not have continued its "aggression against Iraq."

"If those who assume Arab citizenship do not supply America and its partners with bases to facilitate its aggression, America will not be able to do anything more than come for a few hours to strike and disappear," he said.

The above articles merely give a taste of Saddam's capabilities and tenacity. Yet Saddam Hussein who has murdered millions of people was never brought before the War-Crimes Tribunal in Hague. But Slobodan Milosevic who was responsible for a war of self-defense and Yugoslav sovereignty was. While Saddam Hussein, who has killed millions of people, remains in power laughing both at Presidents Bush and Clinton, Slobodan Milosevic must be removed from power before Serbia-Yugoslavia gets a penny in reconstruction aid. This is President Clinton's "diktat." Something's wrong!

Finally, in conclusion of this chapter, why has nothing been done to end the civil war in Sudan. Isn't the genocide of two million black people "ethnic cleansing?" Is this not a holocaust? Why is Omar Bashir or Hassan Turabi of Sudan who are both guilty of this genocide getting off scott free? Isn't the scheduled killing of another 6-8 million blacks in the future by the Muslim government of Sudan a holocaust?

Where was President Clinton when 800,000 Tutsi tribesmen were hacked to death by Hutu tribesmen in Rwanda? What about the 200,000 Catholics on the Island of East Timor slaughtered by the Islamic Indonesian army in 1977?

Why is nothing being said about these and 60 other worldwide ethnic conflicts? Why focus on only those events in which Moslems are the victims and not the perpetrators. What does this say about Israel and the Palestinians? This will be dealt with in a later chapter.

Chapter Four

Background to the Balkans Conflict

One of the reasons for writing this, my second book, is that the historical background provided in the first book regarding Yugoslavia and the Bosnia crisis was very brief, only about six pages. By the time the latest crisis in Kosovo began to develop, I realized that a much more in depth history was needed for the uninitiated reader.

It is ironic that I studied both at New York University and Hebrew University in Jerusalem with Sovietology, East European studies and Balkan studies as my major. I studied this discipline because it was the height of the Cold War between the capitalist west and the communist east, and I thought: "You need to know your enemy to defeat or befriend him." I never really had much opportunity to use what I studied in college to make a living for myself. (Instead, I entered the business world for 15 years.) By the 1990's, communism collapsed and with it Sovietology. Now, all of a sudden, what I studied thirty years ago has become relevant again, but for other reasons.

My minor in college was Spanish and Latin American studies. Similarly, this branch of history was a subject I found very interesting, but neither could it provide for me an income to be spoken of. It was only in 1995 with the writing of "Is Fanatic Islam a Global Threat," that I came to realize the repercussions of the history of these two geographic regions in light of the Islamic Arab invasions from the west, and later, the Islamic Turkish invasions from the east. Historical processes going on for over 1,400 years are continuing today, but most people cannot fathom these processes for a lack of knowledge. It says in the Bible: "My people perish for lack of knowledge." (Hosea 4:6)

Strangely, the common thread linking Russian and Spanish history over the last 1,300 years has been a tradition of war between Christianity on the one hand and Islam on the other. These two geographical spheres bore the brunt of Islamic invasions. The Spanish-Portuguese Iberian peninsula was invaded in 711 AD, by an army of Moors and Arabs coming across the straits of Gibraltar. This invasion reached its apex in France but was turned around at the battle of Poitier by Charles Martel in 732. It wasn't until 1492, however, that the last of the Islamic kingdoms in Spain, Granada, was overwhelmed by Catholics forces and the re-conquest or "reconquista" was completed. These 781 years of struggle with Islam are deeply imbedded in the collective memory of all Spaniards and Portuguese.

Similarly, it was in the year 995 AD that Russia became an official Christian orthodox country with the establishment of its church. The need for establishing the church was to unify the Russian people and to rally the people to defend Russia from the Islamic hordes riding across the steppes, killing, raping and pillaging. The symbol of Moscow is St. George killing the dragon, meaning defeating Islam.

As for Serb history, the Serbs are one of many southern Slavic peoples which originated from further to the north and invaded the area today known as Serbia in the years 675-681AD. They became part of what was then the Byzantine Empire and converted to Orthodox Christianity. Other southern Slavic tribes speaking basically the same language include the Slovenes and Croats who converted to Catholicism and the Bosnians who belonged to a heretical form of Christianity known as the Bogomils. The Bogomils were a sect that arose around the year 1000. Their main tenet was that God had two sons: Christ and Satan. Their founder was a priest called Bogomilu. With the Turkish victory over the Serbs at the Battle of Kosovo field in 1389, the heretical Bosnians, who had been chafing under both Catholic and Serb Orthodox persecution converted over time to Islam and became integrated into the Turkish empire. Indeed, the Turkish system opened its gates to all those who converted to Islam. This included Greeks, Italians, Jews, and Slavic peoples who opted for working with the Turks in order to "advance in life."

The Albanians were the original indigenous inhabitants of the Dalmatian coast. They are not a Slavic people. They were also known in ancient times as the Illyrians. There are some historical theories about the Philistines, who invaded Israel's coastline around 1200 BC, as being of Illyrian ancestry. They were a poor peasant people living in isolated mountainous areas suffering from continuous battles between clans and fell for different periods under the domination of the Venetians, Genoese, and Slavic groups as well.

With the arrival of the Turkish invaders, the Albanians put up a valiant resistance for many decades. Most famous of their leaders was Skanderbeg.   In any event, the Albanians were also overcome by the persistent Turkish invaders and with time about 70% of Albania converted to Islam.

To better understand Serb history, it must be remembered that the Serbs, after their migrations from further north became members of the Byzantine Empire. Therefore, understanding Byzantine history, and more precisely its fall to the invading Ottoman Turks, is critical for setting the stage for what is happening today.

Byzantium, also known as the Eastern Roman Empire abandoned paganism and became Christian as Constantine I ascended to the throne as sole emperor of the Roman Empire in 324. The famous First Ecumenical Council of Nicaea was convened in 325.

Meanwhile, Rome was sacked by Alaric the Visigoth in 410 and by the Vandals in 455, both migrating groups coming down from northern Europe.

Byzantium, meanwhile faced a series of wars which eventually wore it down until it succumbed to the Ottoman Turks in 1453: Persians in 610-638; Avars in 626; Arabs 635-717; Russians in 860 and 941; the Bulgarians in 1017; the break with the Roman Catholic Church in 1054; Hungarians in 1064; Seljuk Turks 1067 and 1071; Catholic crusaders during the four crusades: 1096,1147, 1189, and 1201; and finally, Ottoman Turks from 1300 to 1453.

Serbia's first monarchy was established by Stephen Nemanja in 1180. As an orthodox Christian nation, like Byzantium, it had to face off against the Catholics, due to the break in 1054. This included the Croats to the west, the Slovenes to the northwest, and the Hungarians to the north. Also to the west were the Bosnians who were heretical Bogomils.

In 1201, during the fourth crusade, Constantinople became the target of the Roman Catholic crusaders and was captured in 1204. It wasn't until 1261 that Michael VIII Palaeologus took Constantinople from Latin control and established the dynasty of the Palaelogi. In 1274, Byzantine Emperor Michael came to terms with Pope Gregory X, acknowledging papal primacy and the Roman faith.

Soon after, in 1300, the Ottoman Turkish conquests began, diminishing the Byzantine Empire. In 1329, the Turks captured Nicaea and other cities to become masters of Asia Minor (Anatolia or modern Turkey). In 1354, the Turks took Gallipoli, getting menacingly closer to Constantinople. In 1359, The Turks invaded up to the walls of Constantinople.

Seeing that the city was too fortified to conquer, the Turks turned northwards away from the city and conquered Serbia by defeating the Serbs at the famous battle of Kosovo Field in 1389. This marked the end of the Serbian Empire established in 1180. In 1393, the Bulgarian Empire as well was subjugated by the Ottomans, who held that country for a subsequent 500 years until Bulgaria's War of Independence from Turkey won in 1878.

Now that Constantinople became completely surrounded, Ottoman Sultan Bayazid attacked it but failed. In 1402, Constantinople received a temporary reprieve with the appearance on the scene of the Mongols, led by Timur commonly known as Tamerlane, who defeated the Turks at the Battle of Ankara. But in 1422, the Turks, under the leadership of Murad II again attempted to attack Constantinople but failed. So, in 1430, Turkish forces turned westward to consolidate their hold on the Balkans and captured Salonika.

In 1438, The Council of Ferrara attempted to end the religious schism between East and West in the hope that Christian union might save the Byzantine Empire.

In 1440, the Turks again turned their attention northwards and unsuccessfully besieged Belgrade. But in 1444, they defeated the Bulgarians and their Polish allies killing King Ladislas III of Poland.

In 1452, the Turks built the fortress Remeli Hisar, closing the Bosporus straits to Christian invaders. Finally, Constantinople was besieged by Mehmet II and at last fell to the Turks, ending the Byzantine Empire.

(By the way, it was in this context that Christopher Columbus of Spain decided to travel westwards from Spain not in order to discover America but to find a westward trade route to India and China due to the closure of the eastern trade route by the Turks, by Islam. Christendom was now in a chokehold by the Moslems.

With Columbus's discovery of the New World, two new continents were opened up to Christian settlement, thus overcoming the Islamic stranglehold on Europe. It is never emphasized enough how critical the gold and silver as well as other riches sent back to Europe by the settlers and conquistadores in the new world were to the building of fleets and fielding of armies to fight Islamic armies be they Arab, Turkish or Persian.)

But again, returning to the subject of Serbia, which is at the heart of the Yugoslavia, it needs to be said that after the Turkish victory at Kosovo Field, the Serbs, like all their neighbors, became part of that nebulous, expanding Turkish Empire. The vassal Serbs had to pay taxes and even provide troops to serve in the Turkish army alongside the Moslems. An example of this was Serb participation alongside the Ottoman Turks in the battle against the Mongols in 1402 at Ankara.

In addition, the Turks believed in the system of "divide and conquer." There were over hundreds of years of Turkish control, different Serb vassals chosen to rule over their people in exchange for loyalty to the "Sublime Porte."

The reign of Suleiman the Magnificent (1520-55) marked the summit of Moslem power and prestige. Belgrade was conquered in 1521, Mohacs, the Hungarian version of Kosovo, fell in 1526. The Hungarians would remain under Moslem rule for 150 years. And in 1529, the Turks were now at the gates of Vienna. For more than a century and a half, Vienna stood as the protector of Christian Europe against Moslem forces.

It was during this period that Slovenia and Croatia came increasingly under Austrian and therefore Catholic control, as opposed to the Serbs and Bulgarians who were now isolated behind Islamic, Turkish borders. While the former Slavs were being modernized as Western Europe was emerging from the Renaissance and entering the modern Europe age, the latter remained poor, isolated and left behind in a country which became known as the "sick man of Europe."

The final Turkish attempt at advancing into Europe to further its conquests took place in the second siege of Vienna in 1683. Turkey's defeat in this battle signaled the beginning of the Christian re-conquest of Eastern Europe parallel to the Spanish "reconquista" which was by now completed in 1492.

In 1686, the Hungarians recaptured Budapest from the Turks. As part of the Treaty of Karlowitz of 1699, Turkey lost its control over Hungary after ruling the Magyars 150 years. Hungary, Transylvania, Croatia, and Slavonia now became part of the Austro-Hungarian Empire. Meanwhile, Venice received Morea and Dalmatia. This was all part of the grand alliance of Austria, Venice, Poland, and Russia.

The period of 1699-1812 was one of general decline for Turkey marked by unsuccessful wars with Russia ending with the treaties of Kucuk-Kaynarji–1774, Jassy–1792, and Bucharest of 1812.

Under the leadership of Catherine the Great of Russia, the Russians now got land on the Black Sea and were now the champions of Balkan orthodoxy. The Treaty of Bucharest ceded Bessarabia and Trans-Dniestria to Russian control.

With the rise of Napoleon Bonaparte, France took from Austria and Venice, the lands of Istria, Slovenia, Dalmatia and parts of Croatia. These areas became known as "The Ilyrian Provinces." It was during this brief French control of these Balkan areas that new western ideas of democracy and nationalism were introduced into the Balkans. These ideas would germinate within a few years as would the inspiration for these different Balkan nations to seek independence and nationhood.

However, with the defeat of Napoleon, Austria was now back in control. The Treaty of Vienna of 1815 gave Austria control of the Croats and the Slovenes. Austria now also controlled Vojvodina and its Serb population. These people had fled into the region north of the Sava River to escape Turkish domination and had been permanently settled there by Vienna in an attempt to establish a military frontier defended by local inhabitants. This region thereafter became a vigorous center of Serb national life. The capital was Novi Sad, a city not far from Belgrade, still under Ottoman rule. The Serb Orthodox partriarch lived not far, in Austrian-controlled Karlowitz.

Meanwhile, the Serbs living still under Turkish rule were chafing and rose twice in revolt. The first revolt led by Karageorge, took place between 1804 and 1813. It failed because the much sought after Russian backing failed to materialize. The revolt was brutally suppressed. So, brutally in fact, that another revolt broke out in 1815 under the leadership of Milos Obrenovic. With the Treaty of Akkerman in 1826, the Serbs now wrestled autonomy out of the Turks, though the latter still had some bases in Serbia, the last of which were removed only 1861.

The Russian-Turkish war of 1828-29 ending with the Treaty of Adrianople saw Russian troops at the gates of Constantinople. Serb-autonomy was reconfirmed, Greece became an autonomous tributary state and Rumanian prinicipalities came under Russian protectorship.

But now, France and England became alarmed at Russia's growing might. This became a threat to English colonial aspirations from Europe down into Africa and across to Asia. Too weak a Turkey was considered bad for the western powers, so the Crimean War broke out in 1853-56. English, French and

Turkish troops took the Crimean port of Sevastopol. With the Treaty of Paris, Russian protectorship of the Rumanian principalities came to an end. Rumania received its independence under the leadership of Alexander Cuza in 1861.

But, Russia was not to be deterred. Pan-Slavism, an ideology linking all Slavs with Russia as their protector became the fashion. With an anti-Turkish revolt taking place in Herzegovina in 1775, and a war between Serbia and Montenegro against Turkey, Russia joined the fray in the Russian-Turkish War of 1877-78. At the treaty of San Stefano of 1878, Bulgaria and Serbia finally became independent from Turkey. In 1885, Eastern Rumelia joined Bulgaria and Macedonia now became autonomous under Turkish rule.

In the Balkan wars of 1902-3, 1912 and 1913, Macedonia was divided up between Serbia, Greece and Bulgaria, and the final borders of the Balkans were determined leading up to World War I. By now, Turkey was virtually pushed out of Europe altogether. This signals the end of the Islamic retreat.

In order to understand the present situation in the Balkans as we enter the 21st century, emphasis must now be placed on the struggle between the German-Austrian part of Western Europe and orthodox Eastern Europe in alliance with England, France, and later the US.

As mentioned previously, the Russians were perceived as the protectors of Serbs, Bulgarians, Rumanians and Greeks. The German-Austrian alliance was the defender of Slovenes, the Croats, the Bosnians and the Hungarians.

With the end of WWI, and the defeat of the latter alliance, Romania received Transylvania from Hungary, which itself left the now dissolved Austro-Hungarian Empire. The Slovenian, Croatian, and Bosnian areas became republics together with Macedonia, Serbia and Montenegro to form one united country known as Yugoslavia. Even though Slovenia and Croatia were Catholic, Bosnia was Moslem, and Serbia, Montenegro and Macedonia were mostly orthodox Christian, all six republics spoke the same language known as Serbo-Croatian and all were Slavic peoples.

With the Nazi invasion of World War II, it was decided to "divide and conquer" much as the Turks had done previously in history. The Nazis dissolved Yugoslavia back into its mini components. The Croats and Slovenes who were Catholic felt comfortable with this. And so did the Bosnian Moslems. The Serbs fought back and were targeted by the Nazi war machine, very often with the active assistance of the Croats, led now by the Ustashi nationalist and pro-Nazi movement. Over 100,000 Jews and 500,000 Serbs died at the Nazi concentration camp of Jasenovacs as well as in other concentration camps. Terrible atrocities were committed against the Jews and the Serbs. The Nazis also formed special Moslem brigades of Bosnian and Albanian fighters. Moslem Arabs from the British colony of Palestine also volunteered. Their leader was the Mufti of Jerusalem, Haj Amin el Husseini.

At this point, I want to take the liberty to relate a testimony I received during an interview I was giving at Radio Moscow in Russia in 1994. My interviewer and host, Oleg Gribkov, told me about how ferocious the Moslem soldiers were in Hitler's army at the Battle of Stalingrad in 1942. At that time, there was an alliance of armies from Germany, Hungary, Rumania, Spain, Croatia, Bulgaria, and Bosnia-Albania. When it was decided that the time had come to surrender to Stalin, the only group that refused to surrender were the Moslem soldiers who charged the Russian troops in a last futile attack with bayonets drawn and daggers clenched between their teeth. They were known as Hitler's fiercest fighters.

It is also a known fact that as the Serbs were being "ethnically cleansed" by Hitler, the Nazis were bringing Albanians into Kosovo as it was emptied of its Serbs. This is one of the reasons why Kosovo in 1999 was about 90% Moslem whereas it was about 50% at the end of World War II. (It must be remembered that the Albanians killed 200,000 Serbs in Kosovo in 1915 at the same time that the Turks killed 1,500,000 Armenians in Anatolia.)

With the end of World War II, Yugoslavia was reconstituted under the leadership of the Communist Party headed by

Iosip Broz Tito, an ethnic Croat. Tito believed that Communism would be the system to essentially bury or cement-over all the ethnic hatred that existed between the rival groups in the Yugoslav federation. His dream was to create a new, united Yugoslavia. One of the decisions he took was to take land from what was formally "Greater Serbia" and to give of these Serb lands to the five other constituent republics in order to placate them. Since Tito ruled Yugoslavia with an iron fist, there was really little the Serbs could do to protest.

With the collapse of Communism in the late 1980's came the dismemberment of Yugoslavia in the 1990's with four constituent republics withdrawing and declaring their independence. Two republics, Serbia and its loyal ally throughout history, Montenegro, today are all that is left of Yugoslavia.

It seems that the cement of Communism was cracking and between the cracks the seeds of hundreds of years of ethnic hostilities latent and dormant during the communist period were now germinating.

Slovenia succeeded in breaking away with relative ease. Croatia faced off against Serbia in a war ending with the "ethnic cleansing" of Serbs and Moslems who were forced to leave. Not mentioned is the region of Kraina in Tito's "greater" Croatia that had traditionally been Serb land for 1,300 years. Hundreds of thousands of Serbs were now forced to flee from their homes in Croatia and into Serbia and became refugees. According to Sadako Ogata, UN High Commissioner for Refugees there were half a million refugees of Serbian origin from Bosnia and Croatia who fled to Serbia and Montenegro and are still living as destitute refugees. (International Herald Tribune, Monday, June 14th, 1999)

The Serb feeling in this matter is as follows: Tito gave the Croats land that had been Serb for 1,300 years. As long as Croatia remained part of Yugoslavia, it really didn't matter. But once Croatia decided to quit the Yugoslav federation, Croatia should have given back to the Serbs that which was rightfully theirs. The Croats refused. War ensued. The Serbs were fighting for what they perceived as their land.

This situation repeated itself in Bosnia. Serbs living on lands that had been Serbian for 1,300 years were now Bosnian citizens under what was planned to become an Islamic state under Alija Izetbegovitch. Prime Minister Izetbegovitch wrote his doctoral thesis on how he would take Bosnia, break away from the Yugoslav Federation and turn Bosnia into an Islamic fundamentalist state. The Serb desire is for Serb land to return to Serbia.

This was the situation with the publication of my first book, "Is Fanatic Islam a Global Threat?" My decision to write this book, "Christian Revival for Israel's Survival" was in great part due to the latest crisis in Kosovo.

This war between Albanian Kosovar Moslems and the Serbs is the culmination of centuries of ethnic hatred and contention. What most people throughout the world know not is that Pristina, the capital of the province of Kosovo, is the "Jerusalem" of the Serb people and Serbian Orthodox Church. It has been so for 1,300 years. It is where the Serbian Orthodox Church was founded. There are over 1,000 churches, monasteries and holy sites there. Kosovo has always had a Serb population. To take away Kosovo from Serbia or Yugoslavia is to cut the heart out of that people. To do so and to create an Islamic state in Kosovo, would be like taking away Jewish Jerusalem and giving it to the Palestinian Moslems. For the Serbs, this is as tragic as the Romans expelling the Jews from Jerusalem in 70AD, renaming Jerusalem "Aelia Capitolina," and forbidding the Jews from ever entering their capital of 3,000 years.

Starting with the defeat of the Serb armies at Kosovo Field in 1389, Turkish rule was disastrous to the Serb presence. Turkish soldiers, as well as non-Turkish converts to Islam were systematically settled by the Turks in Kosovo. Later, Hitler's Nazis and allies rewarded the Moslem Albanians by settling them in Kosovo, again at the expense of numerous Serb casualties. After World War II, there was also an illegal influx of destitute people from Albania into the relatively richer Kosovo. The Albanian Kosovars also had a much higher birthrate. On the other hand, there was a Serb exodus from the rural province for more prosperous urban areas of Serbia. The Serb contention also is that during the years when President Iosip Broz Tito was courting Albania's Marxist regime, the Belgrade government settled newcomers from Albania on lands confiscated from the Serbian Orthodox Church.

Serbs who fled Kosovo during World War II were for a time even banned from returning to the province as an overture to the Albanians when the two Communist governments were considering a union.

In today's reality, the KLA, the Kosovar Liberation Army is the outgrowth of a drug-smuggling operation funneling drugs from the Islamic world into the heart of Europe. The Albanians are being armed, supplied and financed by the Islamic world, especially Iran. Osama Ben Laden has an office in Albania. And now the "One World Government" is continuing the pro-Islamic and pro-Nazi system of "divide and conquer," as usual, at the expense of the Serbs.

Ethnic cleansing is horrible regardless of who is perpetrating it on whom. There are no "good guys" in any war. Terrible things have been happening to all national groups in the Balkans for centuries. The Serbs and Russians were allies of the free world fighting Nazism in World War II. Today, the allies of Nazism in World War II have been chosen by the "One World Government" to be the victors.

Russia, the traditional backer of orthodox Christianity in the Balkans is economically in chains to the western powers and therefore impotent. Serbia has little petroleum. Most important of all, the "agenda of the One World Government" together with international Islam and its petrodollar are all that matter. The Serbs, who are faithful Christians, are alone and can be sacrificed according to the "One World Government" agenda. The Serb "Jerusalem" is being handed over to Islam. A new Islamic Albanian state of Kosovo has been created with NATO's bombing the Serbs to smithereens in 72 days.

Many people throughout the world blame Slobodan Milosevic for the troubles taking place in the former Yugoslavia. It still remains to be seen what will come in the aftermath of NATO's massive bombing of the Serb side. Three things were achieved: Firstly, the forging of unity to a man, woman and child behind Milosevic. He became a hero in the eyes of the Serbs, because he was defending to the best of his ability, the true interests of the Serb people. Secondly, the massive dislocation and flight of the Kosovar Albanians from their homes into the Kosovar forests, Albania, Macedonia, Montenegro (which is still part of Yugoslavia!) and other countries. Thousands of Kosovar Albanians as well as Serbs people have died from the bombings and the ensuing civil war. Thirdly, NATO and Russia are now sinking into a quagmire of peacekeeping that will last for many, many years and exact many casualties among the peacekeepers as well as the indigenous populations. The ethnic hatreds are still in place and even enhanced. The murders will still continue, this time with NATO and Russia in the crossfire.

The Serbs, it seems have been defeated. They have lost Kosovo. And the cards are stacked against them in the future as well. The Serb partisans had no tanks, artillery or aircraft in World War II. Yet they pinned down dozens of Nazi divisions in a bloody, guerrilla, standstill war. Could it be that the Serbs, perhaps even with some Russian peacekeeping forces in Kosovo, might end up in renewed conflict with the other western peacekeeping troops as the Moslems take over and expel the Christian Serbs? Could this become a guerrilla operation against NATO similar to the partisan war against the Nazis? How many NATO body bags will be returned to member countries, God-forbid? Could this lead to World War III between orthodox Christians on the one hand and a western-Islamic alliance? Should we not remember that the assassination of Archduke Ferdinand in 1914 is what led up to World War I?

International Piracy in Kosovo

Article by Raphael Israeli in The Jerusalem Post.
"Imagine an increasing Mexican population in southern California, or a growing Arab community in southern France, which would declare its will to secede from the American or the

French heartland, and would use violence and terror to achieve its goal.

Would Mexico or Algeria be entitled to bomb Los Angeles or Marseille in support of the dissidents' claim for independence? If they did, the civilized world would be unanimous in condemning this as an act of international piracy.

This is more or less what is happening in Kosovo today. The Serbs have considered Kosovo the cradle of their culture and ethnic identity for centuries. Over the past decades, due to poverty and misery in neighboring Albania, tens of thousands of (mostly illegal) migrants have infiltrated into Kosovo to seek new opportunities. This is not unlike the process of illegal migration from Mexico to the southwestern states of the US or from North Africa to France.

And yet, those same countries which would not allow an illegal immigrant population to secede politically while tearing away part of the national turf, stand at the forefront of the western effort today not only to de-legitimize the legitimate Serb endeavor to protect its national territory, but use force to achieve that morally and politically questionable goal.

NATO did not bombard Yugoslavia because Serbia rejected peace in Kosovo, but because the West backed the Albanians' demand for self-determination at the expense of their hosts, and insisted on the presence of an international force on the sovereign territory under Belgrade" lawful jurisdiction.

This is something the proud Serbs rejected, exactly as Washington and Paris would oppose any interference of outsiders in their internal matters.

True, there is the moral question of atrocities. The atrocities did not begin with the Serbs. Once the Albanians backed up their demand for independence with violence and terror, what were the Serbs supposed to do? Bow out and withdraw from their sovereign territory? Under conditions of guerrilla warfare, atrocities are bound to happen, on both sides, gory and inexcusable as they be.

If this new form of international piracy is allowed to continue, more foci of unrest will arise at the heart of the West.

Instead of focusing the struggle against the rising threat of fundamentalist Islam (in which the Serbs have stood in the forefront, first in Bosnia and now in Kosovo), the West will make a grave error if it weakens itself in this exercise of self-immolation that is hard to understand, much less to condone."

Finally, the map of the Balkans looks like this. Albania, which used to be the only Moslem country in Europe, now has a sister Moslem country known as Bosnia. In addition, Albanian Kosovars have taken over Kosovo and detached it from Yugoslavia. Kosovo will therefore either merge with Albania or form a second Albanian country in Europe. In addition, there is a big and growing minority of Albanians and Turks in Macedonia, Greece and Bulgaria. There are even still Moslems living in what remains of Yugoslavia. Christianity is on the retreat. Islam is on the march.

Is this a dress rehearsal, a precedent, for what is about to happen to Israel? A struggle over the creation of a Palestinian state has been taking place since the end of World War I. Here, too, two nations are fighting over a small piece of land with its capital Jerusalem. The parallels between the plight of the Serbs and the Israelis are all to clear. The "One World Government" is clearly on the side of Palestinian Moslems because it is subservient to the Islamic global agenda and petrodollar. As I mentioned in my first book, the Dallas Council on World Affairs made it clear to me in April 1991, that Israel would be sacrificed to the Moslems on the "altar of oil." This includes Jerusalem. Perhaps, God forbid, there are those in the corridors of power who think they can tear away the Christian Jerusalem of the Serbs, Pristina, and hand it over to the Moslems. So, too, do they believe they will be able to take away Jewish Jerusalem from the Jews and Christians and give to the Moslems? I will deal with this scenario in the next chapter.

I see the nightmare unraveling before me with the Serbs being made an example of, being sacrificed for oil. Over two million black Christians in the south of Sudan have been killed over the last two decades in a civil war which is nothing less than genocide. Here, too, Islamic Sudan is part of the Islamic global petrodollar agenda. Black blood is just as cheap if not cheaper than Jewish or Christian blood. As with the Jews in the Holocaust, the Blacks are being killed with poison gas and chemicals supplied by Iran and Iraq. I dealt with this in my previous book. Where is President Clinton now? Where is the UN? Where is the "One World Government?"

Over 200,000 Catholics have been slaughtered since 1977 in East Timor by the Indonesian Islamic army. Of course, Indonesia is an oil exporting country. The Coptic Christians of Egypt are being annihilated and forced to flee Egypt. The same has been happening in Lebanon, in Bethlehem, and in Nazareth. Sharia or Islamic law has become the law for everyone in Pakistan, including the Christians. The Christians there are being tortured and slaughtered. Is there not a pattern here? As the sign in the Oval Office of the White House says, "It's the economy, stupid." There seems to be a list or rather blacklist of nations that are obstacles in the way of the "economy", of the perceived global economic agenda. It's not a question of right, but of mammon and might. This, it seems, is how the President of the United States believes. But the God of Abraham, Isaac, and Jacob thinks otherwise as we see in the Bible. God is in control and will sort things out. I would not want to be in the position of the President and those who support the "One World Government."

Chapter 5

Kosovo and Jerusalem

On Saturday night, June 12, 1999, Palestinian Liberation Organization leader, Yasser Arafat, announced that he was calling on NATO to do to Israel what it has done to Yugoslavia in order to end the "Zionist occupation" of Palestinian lands.

Before I deal with my perception of eschatology in the Middle East and the world, I want to review a number of links in the chain of Israel's security and defense that were handled much more in depth in "Is Fanatic Islam a Global Threat?"

We must look back into history. It cannot be emphasized enough that the war in the Middle East is a religious war. It is a war between Islam and Judeo-Christianity. Any lands that have been conquered by Islam can never revert to being "infidel." This is why any peace agreement between Israel and the Palestinians or between the Judeo-Christians and the Moslems in Israel, Lebanon, Egypt, Sudan, Pakistan, Indonesia, or Africa can never be a lasting agreement. This is also true for wars between Moslems and Hindus in the Indian sub-continent or between Moslems and the Chinese in Sinkiang Province of western China.

Yasser Arafat was quoted in a South African mosque immediately after signing the Oslo I accord with Israel in September, 1993, as saying that the agreement with the Jews was only a temporary agreement just as Mohammed's agreement with the tribe of Quraish in the 620's. The agreement was for ten years. Yet Mohammed broke the treaty after two years when he saw he was ready to renew the war against the Jews.

So, too, the Palestinians view their "peace" with Israel as only temporary. When they feel they will be ready to resume war, (with NATO backing) they will.

When I asked my Egyptian-born wife what she thought about the assassination of President Anwar Sadat of Egypt in 1981 by Islamic fundamentalists, she answered: This is a black day for Israel. Mubarak is a warrior, a role model for Egyptian youth. We remember him from the Egyptian media in the 1960's and 70's. He always spoke about how it would be he, the reincarnation of Saladin, victorious Islamic warrior over the Christian crusaders, who would destroy Israel. But he would only attack Israel when he was ready to renew the war against the Jews.

My wife predicted that within twenty years, Egypt would attack Israel. On the surface, it would seem that the peace agreement between Israel and Egypt has been a blessing, and it has been a blessing. Israel's population could not have grown from 3.5 million Jews in 1977 to almost 5 million Jews in the year 2000 without this peace agreement.

But in the spring of 1990, Iraqi dictator Saddam Hussein announced that Iraq had enough biological and chemical weapons to burn half of Israel off the map. In the early summer of 1990, (previous to Iraq's invasion of Kuwait) Iraqi Foreign Minister Tarek Aziz announced after a meeting of the ruling Ba'ath Party in Baghdad that he had Egyptian President Husni Mubarak's signature to an agreement that Egypt would attack Israel two weeks after Israel attacked Iraq. (Probably in reprisal for an Iraqi Scud missile-attack on Israel's cities).

But in August 1990, God Almighty intervened to save Israel from real war by deflecting Saddam's madness away from Israel and toward Kuwait. Kuwait was attacked and occupied by Iraqi forces in six hours setting in motion an international effort to dislodge Saddam's forces from Kuwait. Desert Shield was to last until January 15th, 1991 and Desert Storm until the end of March.

Midrash is a form of Jewish literature dating back almost 2,000 years. Jewish rabbis tried to interpret reasons for unexplained phenomena in the Bible. For example, why did Moses stutter? So a midrashic tale was written about the baby Moses playing on the floor of Pharoah's court at Pharoah's feet. The infant loved to play with Pharaoh's golden crown. At one point, Pharoah's advisers warn him that Moses would take away

Pharaoh's crown and destroy his kingdom. Pharaoh replied, "Nonsense. I will show you." So Pharaoh took a glowing ember from the fireplace and put it down next to the crown. According to the midrashic fable, Moses really wanted to grasp the crown, but God sent an angel to divert Moses' hand away from the crown and to grasp the burning, glowing ember. After sensing the burning coal, Moses naturally put his hand up to his mouth, thus burning his mouth as well. So, now, the Midrash affords all of us an explanation as to why Moses stuttered. Pharaoh then mocked the advisers and said, "You advisers are just as foolish as that child." But baby Moses' life was spared.

So, too, I believe God diverted Saddam's cruel madness away from the Jews and toward Kuwait. There are those who believe that Saddam fell into a trap laid by the "One World Government." US ambassador April Gillespie denies having given Saddam a "green light" to attack Kuwait, but it was reputed by the world media that when Saddam asked April Gillespie what the US would do if he attacked Kuwait, she replied, "Nothing, as long as the oil continues to flow. This is an internal Arab affair."

It must be remembered that the Gulf War was very lucrative for US military hardware manufacturers. There was a price tag attached to any US or allied involvement in dislodging Saddam from Kuwait, a very lucrative price tag. It was not important that hundreds of thousands of innocent people had to die as a result, as long as certain people in the west made bundles of money on weapons sales.

But whatever the reason for Saddam's attack on Kuwait, God deflected the wrath of Satan away from Israel. Even though 39 Scud missiles hit Israel's population centers, only one person died from a direct hit while 27 US military personnel were killed in one Scud hit on a barracks in Dhahran, Saudi Arabia. And that one man killed in Israel died because he refused to go down into the air-raid shelter with his wife and children. I think that is an undeniable proof of God's existence.

Why did Israel not counterattack? According to the media, then Secretary of Defense Caspar Weinberger warned the Israeli Air Force it would be shot out of the skies by US aircraft because he refused to share the air codes with Israel identifying the Israeli aircraft as friendly. I believe the real reason was the Tarek Aziz- Mubarak agreement in writing that Egypt would attack Israel two weeks after Iraq did.

Because the Iraqis attacked Kuwait without consulting or coordinating first with their Egyptian partners, this was like a slap in the face of the "Arab honor" of Egypt. Over a million Egyptian laborers were forced to flee penniless from Iraq and Kuwait back to Egypt at the loss of over $7 billion to the Egyptian economy. (Attention US Taxpayers: The US later forgave Egypt of $7 billion in Egyptian debts to the US.)

The Iraqi attack on Kuwait was like two thieves planning to rob a bank together at 2PM in the afternoon and meanwhile, the first thief robs a bank all by himself at 10AM. (The original plan was for Iraq and Egypt to attack Israel. Meanwhile Iraq attacked Kuwait first without consulting with Egypt.) The rhetorical question is: Will the second thief rob the bank together with the first thief at 2PM when the police are already in hot pursuit of the first thief after the former robbed the bank at 10 AM. Highly unlikely, I believe.

So Israel was spared a terrible war in 1991. Some estimates are that had Israel retaliated in self-defense and attacked the Iraqi missile bases at H2 and H3 in western Iraq, Israel would have sustained over 800 casualties. But the question here is would the Arab-American coalition have collapsed with a general Arab assault on Israel had it retaliated against the Iraqi scud attacks? I believe the answer is yes.

On the surface, it would seem that my wife was wrong about her prediction regarding an Egyptian attack on Israel, because we have had peace with Egypt since 1979. But the agreement to attack Israel was there in place. It was only because God acted supernaturally to divert Saddam Hussein's madness away from Israel that war was averted.

Then in November 1993, it was revealed by American military liaison officers training the Egyptian army in its desert that the Egyptian maps were pointing to an attack on Israel.

In October 1994, a full year before the assassination of Prime Minister Yitzhak Rabin, an article appeared in the Egyptian magazine, "Rose el-Youssef" containing interviews with former War Minister Huwaidi and present War Minister Tantawi

containing two dubious quotes showing Egypt's tactical intentions regarding Israel:

1. Huwaidi: War with Israel is a certainty and Egypt is
ready.

2. Tantawi: Even though Israel has nuclear weapons,
Egypt will know how to cut off the arm of the enemy when the
time comes.

How could the Egyptian military leaders speak like this at
the height of the "peace process" and during the lifetime of
Yitzhak Rabin if peace was their intention? How could "Rose
el-Youssef" print such quotes without the express permission of
Husni Mubarak himself?

It must be remembered that Desert Storm-Desert Shield
took place during the term of Prime Minister Yitzhak Shamir.
There were those who contend that had Shamir won the elections in 1992, war would most definitely have broken out between Israel and its neighbors.

But as fate would have it, as God would have it, Yitzhak
Rabin won the elections together with the Labor (socialist) Party.
Again, I believe that God prevented war between Israel and its
neighbors. Now there was a new impetus to what was perceived
as the "peace process". The Oslo I & II Agreements were reached
with the Palestinians. A peace treaty was signed with King
Hussein of Jordan. And it seemed Israel was ready to hand over
the entire Golan Heights to Syria.

Why is it, then, that Prime Minister Yitzhak Rabin did not
return the Golan Heights to Syria? It seems that Rabin had
hypothetically asked Syrian President Hafez al-Assad what kind
of a peace would Israel receive in return for the Golan Heights.
Assad seems to have thought that this was a sign of readiness
on the part of Rabin to return all of the Golan as well as to
salients of territory in Israel proper conquered by the Syrian
army in 1949 during Israel's Independence War.

Rabin, it seems, was ready to offer the full Golan Heights
right down to the lakeshore of Kinneret (The Sea of Galilee).
What Rabin was not ready to surrender were two salients, one
to the west of the Jordan River at Tel Katzir and the second
salient near the junction of the borders of Israel, Jordan and
Syria where there are, at present, crocodile farms known as

Mevo Hama. These two salients belonged to Israel according to the international boundaries established by the UN in 1947. Rabin was ready to return the Golan Heights in entirety, but not the two Israeli salients because they never belonged to Syria de jure but had been conquered de facto by the Syrians in 1949. It was for this reason primarily that the Golan talks failed. When the Syrians demand a resumption of the negotiations at the point at which they were discontinued, the meaning is that the Syrians want the two salients in addition to the Golan Heights. They want the armistice lines of 1949, not the international borders. Rabin believed in peace, true peace, but Hafez al-Assad, if he believed in true peace would have agreed to what he considered his territory but not Israeli territory conquered in 1949 by Syrian forces.

Unfortunately, any withdrawal from the security zone in south Lebanese territory can only happen in conjunction with an overall peace agreement between Israel and Syria, because Syria totally dominates Lebanon.

Yet Syria is in no rush. Hafez el-Assad has been quoted as saying the following:

1. "We have lost five wars against Israel. We can afford to lose 6 wars, 7 wars, or 99 wars. All we need is the 100th war and no more Israel.

2. "It took us 200 years to expel the Crusaders. The Israelis have only been around 50 years. We can wait another 150 years.

3. "Any Arab leader (referring to the king of Jordan, or to Palestinian leader Yasser Arafat) who surrenders even one inch of holy Jerusalem soil to the Israelis is a traitor. And we know the destiny of traitors in the Arab world."

The problem when dealing with Hafez el-Assad is that the Golan Heights is not the problem. Neither is Lebanon the problem. The problem is Jerusalem. There can be no peace without the total devolution of 100% of the territories that Israel was forced to take in wars of self-defense in 1967 & 73.

UN Resolutions 242 and 338 call on Israel to return lands taken during these two wars. These resolutions known as the "land for peace formula" never said that Israel had to return all the lands it was forced to take. On the contrary, these resolutions say that Israel will "negotiate with its neighbors for secure, recognized, and defensible boundaries." It is clear from this that there was to be no return to the 1967 boundaries. Both former Israeli Foreign Minister Abba Eban and former Secretary of State Henry Kissinger have said that the June 5th 1967 Israeli borders were "Auschwitz" extermination camp borders. They were borders that could not be defended by Israel. Israel needed new secure, recognized, and defensible boundaries.

It is my belief that due to the Labor Party replacing the Likud party in power in 1992 and until its fall in 1996, peace was maintained, and war was postponed. The Arab-Islamic coalition could not attack Israel without the politically correct circumstances. It is true that there was a price to be paid: The Oslo I & II Agreements.

In May 1996, faithful to the vicissitudes of Israeli politics, the Likud was back in power, this time led by Benjamin Netanyahu. As a "Middle East Observer," I was fearful, again of circumstances mitigating a new round of war between Israel and its neighbors. Yet, during the election campaign preceding the May vote, Netanyahu pledged to continue the "peace process." He promised he wouldn't scuttle the Oslo Accords.

Yet, in the summer of 1996, the Egyptian army went on its massive Badr 96 maneuvers. Similarly, the Syrian army moved different army units from Lebanon into the Golan Heights to confront Israel and carried out intensive maneuvers of its own.

In November 1996, I returned home to Israel after a few months of lectures in the US. November was a month that I was committed to being available on the duty roster for the IDF spokesman's office as part of my yearly reserves.

During the second week of November, I received an unusual call from a Christian believer in the US who called to warn Israel about information he had received in real time about Syrian, Iraqi, and Egyptian troop movements. A war was about to break out between Israel and its Arab neighbors.

On December 10th, 1996 the Task Force on Terrorism & Unconventional Warfare of the US House of Representatives in Washington, D.C. came out with a report called: "Approaching the New Cycle of Arab-Israeli Fighting" confirming the information I had received from this Christian believer a month previously. This report may be found at http://www.cmep.com/report.htm.

Among the findings of this congressional report were:

1. Syria was preparing for a surprise military attack on Israel.

2. Iraqi troops were streaming across the border into Syria at the Abu Kamal border crossing as reinforcements to the Syrians.

3. Egyptian troops were preparing to enter the fray if called upon. Cairo was encouraging the resumption of calls for war at the political level. Brig. Gen. (Ret.) Mohammed Muawad Gad al-Moula was permitted to establish a new political party committed "to revive the 'victorious spirit' of the October 1973 War." Al-Moula told the semi-official al-Ahram daily, "We have to prepare for a fresh confrontation with Israel."

4. Palestinian soldiers/policemen with tens of thousands of AK-47 machine guns and other weapons in violation of the Israeli-Palestinian peace accords were ready to carry the battle into the streets and cities of Jewish Israel.

The reason for the readiness to face war, as opposed to the reluctance shown previously, is the Muslim world's reading of Israel. Indeed, most senior leaders (especially in Damascus, Tehran, Baghdad and Cairo) are convinced that Israel is falling apart - collapsing from within in a unique state of self-confusion, of having lost the WILL to fight and survive. The rise of militant Islam as the primary motivating factor of the Arab public has already reached unprecedented levels. The Arabs and the Iranians are convinced they can deter an American cover for Israel.

It is because of this as well as US pressure, I believe, that Benjamin Netanyahu was forced to sign the Hebron Accord of February 1997 by which Israel withdrew from 80% of Hebron and handed it over to the Palestinian Autonomy. This accord was a major reason for Netanyahu's loss of support in the Likud, religious, and nationalist camps. It was a cause of Netanyahu's loss in the elections of May 1999 in which Labor returned to power under Ehud Barak. Again, another vicissitude in Israeli politics. But, at the last minute, I believe, the Hebron Accord postponed a new Arab-Israeli war in the Middle East yet another time.

It was this same US-Arab pressure at the Wye Plantation Talks in 1999 to which Netanyahu succumbed, which caused his former nationalist-religious bloc supporters to vilify him and breakaway to form the national bloc under Benny Begin. Yet this capitulation forestalled a war in the Middle East. The bottom line the world is dictating to Israel is this: Capitulate or face a war with all the Arab and Islamic world. The US will not stand with Israel any more. Israel is all alone if it doesn't do what the "One World Government" tells it to do, regardless of the price. All of this was told to me in April 1991 at the Dallas Council of World Affairs.

Since Israel fulfilled 91% of UN Resolutions 242 and 338 by returning the Sinai a third time to Egypt in 1981. Since it fulfilled 2% more by returning half of the Golan Heights to Syria during the disengagement agreements brokered by then Secretary of State Henry Kissinger in June 1974. Since it returned lands to King Hussein of Jordan for a peace treaty in 1994. And since 60% of Gaza and 40% of Judea and Samaria have been already handed over to the Palestinian Autonomy under Yasser Arafat by July 1999, Israel has already fulfilled, in effect, 97% of UN Resolutions 242 and 338.

Any talk against Israel that it does not want peace or is intransigent is fallacious and contrary to UN Resolutions which it has already fulfilled by 97%. Where is the compromise from the Islamic-Arab side? They want the full 100% and more. Now, they have begun demanding UN Resolution 181 of 1947 as a basis for negotiations, which means basically the destruction of Israel. And the Palestinians want NATO to serve Islam and the Palestinians in the destruction of Israel.

At the time of the writing of this book in June 1999, Prime Minister-elect Ehud Barak of the Labor Party is suggesting postponing the implementation of parts of the Wye Plantation Accord signed by Netanyahu and to go on to the final status talks. The logic behind this is: if more land is given to the Palestinians as agreed upon by the Wye Plantation, but there is no agreement on final status talks, then war is still imminent with the

Palestinians. Whatever land given to the Palestinians will be used as jump off points against Israel. The Palestinians want Wye implemented first. A bird in the hand is worth two in the bush or a hundred in the air. This will be Barak's first test with the Palestinians.

But Ehud Barak has other hurdles to be cleared with the Palestinians. He has said that Jerusalem will never be re-divided. The IDF will never retreat from the Jordan River, meaning no territory contiguity between the Palestinian entity and Jordan. No Arab army will be allowed between the Jordan River and the Mediterranean Sea. The Jewish settlements or communities in Judea, Samaria and Gaza, totalling a population of 180,000 will not be dismantled except for maybe just a few. All these points are totally rejected by the Palestinian-Arab-Islamic side.

Even though Ehud Barak was supported entirely by President Clinton and the "One World Government," I believe that these foreign supporters do not realize that Ehud Barak is an Israeli patriot, a tough negotiator and the most decorated man in Israel's military history. I don't believe he's a pushover, and I don't think the Arabs will be satisfied by any means. This I'm afraid will lead inevitably to a war.

In 1998, the UN passed the notorious "war criminal" laws in Rome, Italy, tailor-made for any politician waging a national war of self-defense, sovereignty, and the survival of his people. In the Balkan war between Yugoslavia and the Albanian Kosovars, Slobodan Milosevic became the first war criminal indicted by the Hague. But it is my contention that these "war criminal" laws were created for any Israeli leader at that time in which the Moslem-Palestinian Arabs rose up against the Jews and Israel. At that time, Netanyahu or Barak will immediately be branded by the "community of nations" as war criminals while Yasser Arafat gets the Nobel Peace Prize. This is because Israel, like Yugoslavia just is not part of the "One World Government" pro-Islamic, pro-petroleum agenda. The difference also is that Israel does not have orthodox-Christian Russia as its defender like the Serbs. We have God. A Christian revival and some allies marching with us would really be nice as well.

Chapter Six

Islamic Threat Update

Before getting into the concluding Chapter VII - Eschatology, I thought it would be good to provide a collections of newspaper articles similar to what I did in my first book "Is Fanatic Islam a Global Threat?" These articles are a summary of the Islamic-non-Islamic warfare endemic throughout the world, and about which Christians and other non-Muslims need to be informed. Again, just as I explained in Chapter IV regarding 1400 years of Islamic wars with Byzantium and the Balkans, what is happening now throughout the world is a continuing manifestation of that same war with many nations and religions.

The following articles either appeared after the publication of my first book or were excluded from it due to the lack of space.

The first selections deal with the Islamic harassment and persecution of Christians in the Holy Land.

GOVERNMENT REPORT: PALESTINE AUTHORITY INTENSIFYING BID TO CONTROL CHURCHES

Article by Steve Rodan from Jerusalem Post English language daily October 4, 1998.

"The Palestinian Authority has intensified its effort to control Christian churches in Israel as part of its campaign to acquire their extensive landholdings in the country and gain influence in the West, a government report says.

The report, drafted by security officials for Cabinet review, says the PA effort began with its takeover of churches in Bethlehem, including the Church of Nativity, and has now extended to churches and Christian sites in Jerusalem. These include the Church of the Holy Sepulchre and the Church of Mary Magdalene.

The PA effort is focused on gaining control over the Greek Orthodox Patriarchate in Jerusalem and the Greek Catholic Bishopric in the Galilee.

The drive to dominate the Greek Patriarchate is regarded as most alarming because of the church's vast holdings in the western part of Jerusalem, including land on which the Knesset and many government buildings are located. The Greek Catholics control considerable property in the north of Israel.

'The PA's efforts to take control over the patriarchate consist of a three-pronged approach encompassing the public, legal and political spheres,' the report said.

The PA campaign is being waged by the newly formed Orthodox Congress composed of associations that administer the community's churches, cemeteries, cultural and educational institutions. It is headed by Kamal Ferah of Nazareth.

The report says the Congress is working to create a union of Orthodox Palestinian Christians with two leading PA figures, Marwan Barghouti, West Bank Fatah leader, and Ramzi Khouri, personal secretary to PA Chairman Yasser Arafat.

Over the past four months, the report says, the Congress has demonstrated against the Patriarchate in Ramallah and Amman, with its leaders accusing church leaders of selling property to Israelis. The Congress is also demanding the establishment of a public council to oversee Patriarchate properties and assets.

'The Greek priests who run the Patriarchate have been subjected to threats,' the report says. 'There are reports of plans by the Congress to break in and seize documents and deeds of ownership.'

The PA attempts to wrest control of the Greek Orthodox Church from the patriarchate come as leading PA officials, particularly Faisal Husseini, the minister responsible for Jerusalem, have warned that the Palestinians are preparing to lay claim to large portions of western Jerusalem.

The report says the PA is also trying to gain control over the Armenian Patriarchate and the Franciscan Order, which controls Catholic sites on behalf of the Vatican.

'The PA has used its indirect control over the Church of the Nativity in Bethlehem as a means of influencing the Greek Orthodox and Armenian Patriarchs, through which it impacts on the political positions of the Greek government and the European Union,' the report says.

Ibrahim Kandelaft, head of the PA's Christian affairs department, could not be reached for comment.

Several Jerusalem churches and patriarchates have already turned what the report terms Palestinian. These include the Latin Patriarchate, headed by Michel Sabah and his deputy, Bishop Kamal Batisch; the Anglican Bishopric, headed by Bishop Riah Abu assal; the Lutheran Bishopric, headed by Bishop Munir Yunan and the Greek Catholic Bishopric of Jerusalem, headed by Archbishop Lutfi Laham.

Latin Patriarch Criticizes Israel

Article by Haim Shapiro in the Jerusalem Post of Wednesday, December 23rd, 1998.

Israeli authorities are ultimately responsible for tension and conflicts between Moslems and Christians, both in Israel and the Palestinian Authority, Latin Patriarch Michel Sabbah claimed yesterday in a Christmas message.

At the same time, a close aide to the patriarch named a Likud official as being personally responsible for creating unrest between Moslems and Christians in Nazareth.

Sabbah, stressing the Christian-Moslem tension for the first time, said that Israeli fears over security had impeded the peace process, limiting Palestinian freedom of movement and space to grow, and in turn creating nervousness and tension between individuals and families.

However, he also said that the PA was doing nothing to control inter-religious tension either.

In the PA, fights have erupted between Christians and Moslems in what were once mostly Christian towns such as Beit Sahur and Ramallah. According to Patriarchate spokesman Wadie Abunassar, these were ordinary conflicts between neighbors that were interpreted as inter-religious battles.

Tension in Nazareth relates to an area formerly occupied by a school near the Basilica of the Annunciation, on which the municipality had planned to build a plaza for the year 2000, but which Moslems had occupied, claiming it as the site of a former mosque.

In the recent municipal elections there, the Hadash (Communist) mayor was re-elected, while the Islamic List won a majority of seats on the municipal council. Following a stormy council meeting last week, where those involved failed to agree on a coalition, rioters attacked shops with Christmas decorations and seven people were injured.

Regarding Nazareth, the patriarch said that 'a foreign hand is fomenting discord.' When asked by reporters if he was referring to the Israeli government, he said he was not, adding that the 'foreign hand' was everyone who was interested in fomenting tension. However, he added that it was the responsibility of the government to control the situation.

Later Abunassar told reporters that it was Likud Arab affairs advisor Danny Greenberg who had exacerbated the tension in Nazareth, in an attempt to gain votes for his party. In response, Greenberg said that he had not been involved in the situation for the past year and thus did not understand why such a charge should be made against him.

In reaction to the patriarch's statement, Uri Mor, director of the Religious Affairs Ministry's department for Christian communities, said that the government and the Ministry saw any attack by one religious community on another as serious and worked to ease such tensions. However, Mor angrily rejected any attempt by Sabbah or the leader of any other Christian community to say that Israel was to blame for Moslem attacks on Christians.

Mor added that Internal Security Minister Avigdor Kahalani had personally supervised police action following the attacks last week in Nazareth.

Moslems Attack Christians Celebrating
Easter in Nazareth

Article by Haim Shapiro in the Jerusalem Post of Monday
April 5, 1999.

Brawls between Christians and Moslems in the morning
and evening marred Easter festivities in Nazareth yesterday,
leaving seven people wounded, 30 cars smashed and the town's
main street closed for several hours.

In the evening, police arrested six Moslem stone-throwers
and fired tear gas after firebombs were thrown at them, police
said.

The violence began early yesterday morning when Christian worshipers leaving a church near the historic market encountered Moslem worshipers leaving a temporary mosque set
up in a square which is being occupied by Islamic activists.

The square, on which a school building formerly stood, had
been slated by the municipality for a plaza serving pilgrims arriving for the year 2000, when Islamic activists occupied it nearly
a year ago, claiming it as the site of a former mosque.

Thousands of young Moslem men gathered at the disputed
site near the Church of the Annunciation. Some hurled insults
and curses at Christian worshipers leaving the church, where
Roman Catholic tradition holds that the Angel Gabriel appeared
before Mary and told her she was pregnant.

Other youths, wielding clubs, smashed windshields of cars
with crosses dangling from the mirrors.

About 150 policemen were brought in to end the morning
fighting. At one point, a group of policemen stood and watched
as Moslem youths smashed the window of a Mercedes. There
were no arrests then, said police spokeswoman Linda Menuhin.

The clashes were a repeat of similar violence that took place
there the week before Christmas, when several shops with
Christmas decorations had their windows smashed.

The town has been in a state of unrest since the municipal
elections, which resulted in Mayor Ramez Jeraise of the secular

Hadash party being reelected, while the Islamic list won a majority of the municipal council seats.

The prime minister's adviser on Arab affairs, Motti Zaken, met with Christian and Moslem notables in Nazareth and agreed to meet Thursday to discuss Moslem claims.

Nazareth Mosque Agreement Reached

Article by Ben Lynfield and Haim Shapiro in the Jerusalem Post of April 6th, 1999.

After two days of violence in Nazareth, Mayor Ramez Jeraise has agreed not to block the building of a mosque on a site next to the Church of the Annunciation, a mediator who brokered an agreement between Jeraise and Moslem leaders, said last night.

'The Municipality will not prevent the erection of the mosque when an agreement is reached between the overseers of Islamic endowments and the Israel Lands Authority,' said Mohammed Zeidan, chairman of the Follow-up Committee of the Arab Citizens in Israel. "It is clear according to the agreement reached that there will be a mosque.'

The Municipality had envisioned the area as a Venetian-style plaza for Christian pilgrims.

The agreement comes a day after 12 people were injured in Christian-Moslem violence, and was intended by Arab Israeli leaders to calm tempers in Nazareth.

Christian leaders seemed dismayed by the situation and, in an unprecedented move, patriarchs of the major Christian communities, meeting in Jerusalem last night, decided to close their churches in Nazareth today and tomorrow to protest 'the fact that numerous Christians were injured and insulted' during Sunday's violence.

The patriarchs protested over what they termed 'the inadequate measures' taken by the authorities to ensure safety. They also threatened to repeat the closure if necessary and urged their followers to act 'with Christian love to all those who have attacked us.'

The center of Nazareth was shut down yesterday by a general strike called as a show of strength by the Islamic movement. Channel 1 reported that there were stone throwing incidents.

Helmeted riot police urged residents over loudspeakers to remain indoors as hundreds of Moslem activists gathered at a downtown protest then set up at the site where the movement wants to erect the mosque. AP reported.

Sammy Smooha, a Haifa University sociologist, said that tensions between the two communities are not limited to the mosque issue, have been mounting for several years, and are likely to persist.

According to Smooha, Moslems, who comprise a majority in Nazareth, are bitter at not enjoying economic and political power that reflects their numerical strength.

'The Moslems are not doing very well socio-economically and in terms of jobs, compared with the Christians,' said Smooha. 'The elite is mostly Christian, but the Christians have lost their majority due to a low birth-rate and emigration.'

Speaking before last night's agreement, Smooha added: 'They might strike a deal, but in the long run friction will continue under the surface. This is true not just in Nazareth, but in other locales where Christians are doing well compared to the Moslems. The Moslems would like to get their share.'

Two Shops Firebombed in Nazareth Violence

Article of Associated Press appearing in Jerusalem Post of Thursday, April 8th, 1999.

Two shops, one owned by a Christian and the other by a Moslem, were firebombed and damaged yesterday in renewed sectarian violence in Nazareth.

"Things are getting out of hand... The city is a mess after a year of incitement on sectarian basis," said Suhail Diab, spokesman for Nazareth's municipality.

Violence between Christians and Moslems erupted Sunday over a downtown plot of land near the church of the Annunciation where Christian tradition says the Angel Gabriel told Mary she was pregnant.

The Christian Mayor Ramez Jeraise, backed by the government, wants to build a Venetian-style plaza next to the church in time for the millennium celebrations. Moslem activists claim the land belongs to the Islamic Trust and want to build a large mosque at the site.

Yesterday, the Church of the Annunciation and all other churches in the city of 60,000 remained closed for a second straight day in protest over the violence.

In clashes Sunday, more than a dozen were injured, 30 cars damaged and 11 people arrested.

On Tuesday night assailants hurled a firebomb into a clothing store owned by a Christian, Gabi Laham, who said he suspected Moslem activists were behind the attack. A store owned by a Moslem was also torched.

Diab said he fears sectarian strife will permanently poison the relations between the Moslem majority and the Christian minority.

After municipal elections in November, snags arose over ambitious plans to give the city a facelift for the millenium.

The Islamic movement for the first time won a majority in the city council after making the construction of the mosque next to the church a key issue of the campaign.

Jeraisi was narrowly re-elected but has been unable to form a ruling coalition.

On Holy Ground

Article by Larry Derfner in the Jerusalem Post of Friday, April 16th, 1999

The young woman in Nazareth's Christian Travel Agency was startled when a visitor walked in unannounced this week. The agency's front windows were boarded up after having been smashed by Moslem rioters on the night before Easter.

"It isn't safe here anymore," the woman said, explaining her fearful reaction. This was the third time the office had been trashed by Moslems in recent months, she said. She would not give her name.

The agency is on Rehov Hagalil, Nazareth's main thoroughfare. Right behind Hagalil is the huge black-domed Church of the Annunciation, the holiest church in Israel after Jerusalem's Holy Sepulchre, and the largest church in the Middle East.

In front of the church, facing Hagalil, is a giant black tent that serves as a makeshift mosque. This is the flash point of a conflict that has overtaken this city of some 50,000 Moslems and 25,000 Christians - the largest Arab city in Israel, the place where, according to Christian tradition, Jesus lived nearly 2,000 years ago.

The mosque is named "Shehab a-Din" after the warrior whose burial site is nearby. Shehab a-Din was the nephew of Saladin, the Islamic leader who defeated the Crusaders in the 12th century.

Devout Moslems claim that many other ancient graves of Moslem "martyrs" lie under the ground where the tent stands, which makes it holy Moslem land that rightfully belongs not to its current owner, the Israel Lands Administration, but to the Waqf. They want to build a great mosque there.

The Nazareth municipality, led by Hadash Mayor Ramez Jeraise, a Christian, is unconvinced that the land - except for the quarter-dunam surrounding Shehab a-Din's tomb - has any religious significance. They planned to build a sparkling plaza on the remaining land to accommodate Christian pilgrims for the millenium.

Because of the recent violence, however, construction of the plaza was halted.

A compromise solution is being sought. With millions of Christian pilgrims expected to visit Nazareth over the coming year, a government source said the General Security Service is convinced that if the dispute is not resolved, Moslem violence will intensify.

"There's almost no doubt that justice is on the side of the Christians," the source said. "But at the same time, even the city's Christians, along with the mayor, want to see a compromise reached that will calm the city. Otherwise, the situation in Nazareth will become untenable."

Some 20 Moslem "guards" sleep in the tent surrounded by the green flags of the fundamentalist Islamic Movement. Thousands of Moslems pray there every Friday.

The young imam of the mosque, Nazaem Abu Sle'em, said he has nothing against the church's dominating precsence nearby, and even welcomes the masses of Christian pilgrims due for the millennium.

But if Moslems are not allowed to build a mosque on the site, Abu Sle'em warned, "There is no way that things will be quiet here for the millennium. Do you expect us to allow holy Moslem land, land where revered Moslems were buried centuries ago, to be used for tourists to come and dance upon?"

Next door to the travel agency, a shoe store owned by Christians was also boarded up after its windows were broken. No one was inside. Numerous stores and cars along Hagalil had been smashed and vandalized by Moslem rioters at Easter.

A number of people were injured. George Sheiny, a Christian owner of two clothing stores on Hagalil, said that even a Moslem merchant who tried to protect his Christian neighbors was set upon and beaten by rioters.

Like the travel agency, Sheiny's stores have been attacked three times in recent months, he said. "I drive around here every night at midnight, or one o'clock, to make sure there's no trouble. My sons and daughters work here, and I worry whenever they go out that something's going to happen to them," said Sheiny, 50.

Like other Nazareth residents, he said the conflict over the land is political, spured by "interest groups", and has not harmed relations between ordinary Christians and Moslems, who've lived together in this city for centuries.

"Most of my friends are still Moslems," he said.

A Christian employee in the store, who did not give his name, noted that when Moslem rioters recently tried to vandalize a statue of the Virgin Mary in a local park, Moslem and Christian neighbors joined together to stop them.

Fundamentalist Moslems in the city claim the Easter rioting was provoked by Christians who first attacked the guards sleeping in the mosque. But Christians, along with Moslem supporters of the secular Hadash party, say there was no such attack, and that the Moslem extremists were the sole assailants.

Police spokesmen said the knife and rock fights, torching of cars, and the rest of the general mayhem was initiated by Moslems, but that Christians later retaliated. "in rough proportions, about two-thirds of the attacks were committed by Moslems against Christians, the other third by Christians against Moslems," said police spokesman Moshe Berkowitz.

He said investigators never determined which side started the violence on Easter night. All told, about 50 people have been arrested, and a roughly equal number have been injured - though none seriously.

Mohammed Nasser, a secular Moslem who owns one of the many tourist-oriented Middle Eastern restaurants on Hgalil, tried to downplay the violence, saying it was committed by "young boys trying to imitate the intifada". He also maintains that "both sides took part."

Nasser favors letting the Moslem fundamentalists build their mosque because "it keeps the young men off the streets. Otherwise they'll wander around unemployed, taking drugs. There is a saying: 'A Man who fears God is not to be feared.'"

Another secular Moslem man, who did not give his name, called the Moslem protesters "fanatics." But he, too, thought their claim to the land is justified, and favored allowing the mosque to be built "for the sake of keeping the peace."

On Hagalil and the adjacent streets, Christian tour groups were strolling and visitng the various churches. They seemed unafraid. When asked, however, if the violence has deterred Christian pilgrims from coming to Israel, the woman in the travel agency said that since Easter, Christian tour groups from the US, Turkey and Ireland have canceled their reservations, citing the danger as their reason.

A high-level Christian source in the city asked, "If Christians in France, Italy and the rest of the world see in the media that Moslems are attacking Christians in Nazareth, do you think they're going to want to travel here?"

The dispute over the site, which has been going on for a year and a half, has reached as high as the Vatican. Cardinal

Roger Etchegarray, overseer of the Vatican's millennial celebrations, told Israeli officials on a recent visit that the Church strongly opposed construction of a mosque.

The conflict has also preoccupied the government. Citing Ethegarray's remarks, Avi Blustein, director-general of the Religious Affairs Ministry, urged Tourism Minister Moshe Katsav not to concede to Moslem demands because it would lead to "additional attempts at extortion." Katsav holds the cabinet's Arab affairs portfolio.

Blustein's letter to Katsav was blasted as "'racist'" by Salman Abu Ahmad, leader of the Islamic Movement's bare majority on the Nazareth municipal council.

Shortly after Blustein made his position public, he was stripped of all his responsibilities and ordered by Religious Affairs Minister Eli Suissa to stop interfering in the matter.

Katsav, however, came out in favor of the Moslems' demands. In a Channel I interview last Friday, he said it is only Christian opposition that keeps the government from letting the Moslems have the land.

Jeraise, in turn, called Katsav's statement "a miserable one, and very dangerous." The mayor said Moslems in the tent have referred to him ominously at "Salman Rushdie," and accused him of collecting bones from old Moslem graves supposedly found on the disputed land, and tossing them onto a garbage dump.

"This is a call for my blood. Some violent fanatic could hear these statements and try to act on them," Jeraise said, noting that death threats against him have become commonplace.

In the Islamic Movement's office on Hagalil, Abu Ahmad said he, too, has been getting frequent death threats, and that a firebomb was thrown at his brother's home.

Abu Ahmad, 44, a civil engineer with a degree from the Technion, did not look at all like the stereotypical image of an Islamic Movement leader. Clean-shaven, he was dressed in a business suit and tie. His office was spare except for the framed photographs of mosques on the walls.

"As far as the public's attitude toward this issue goes, the election result speaks for itself," he said. The dispute utterly dominated the November 10 municipal elections in Nazareth, in which the Islamic Movement rose from three seats to 10, and Hadash fell from 11 seats to nine.

Said Jeraise: "I thought that people wouldn't be stirred by emotional religious incitement, but I was wrong."

Jeraise, however, defeated Abu Ahmad for mayor 52.5 to 47.5 percent. The resultant division of power has been insuperable. The one council meeting held since the elections ended when a brawl broke out between Islamic Movement and Hadash supporters.

Eli Suissa, who is also interior minister, is considering disbanding the council, appointing an interim management board to run the city, and calling new elections in the hope that the Islamic Movement-Hadash deadlock may be broken.

The conflict over the land has also entered the national election campaign.

Jeraise accused the Likud, Shas, and United Torah Judaism of trying to win over Moslem voters by supporting the construction of the mosque. But Motti Zaken, Arab affairs adviser in the Prime Minister's Office countered: "If that were true, we could have just given the Moslems the land a long time ago."

Jeraise said a key Likud campaign official had tried to win the Islamic Movement's backing with promises that the land would eventually be given to the Waqf. A government source, however, noted that the Likud had fired the campaign official in question a year ago over this matter. The mayor also claimed that Suissa's talk of disbanding the municipal council is part of Shas's campaign to attract Arab voters. (Suissa heads Shas's electoral campaign in the Arab sector.)

If a new election is held, the rising Islamic Movement could win the mayor's seat, and a larger majority on the council, and thereby have the power to build its mosque in front of the church.

Deputy Housing and Construction Minister Meir Porush, leader of United Torah Judaism, recently visited the Moslems in their tent and declared that they are entitled to build a mosque there, because there are so many churches and relatively few mosques in Nazareth.

Abu Ahmad, however, denies that national politics has anything to do with the dispute. "The Islamic Movement will not trade its supporters' votes for this land, which is holy land that belongs to the Wakf," he declared.

In the Knesset election, he added, the movement's supporters will naturally vote for the Islamic Movement, which is running on a joint list with the Democratic Arab Party. However, he said, in the race for prime minister, the movement is still undecided.

Katsav has proposed seven different compromise solutions, including one that would allow Moslems to build a mosque on the land in front of the church - but a mosque of modest dimensions.

Abu Ahmad, who called Katsav's remarks on Channel 1 "a ray of light," said such a compromise might be acceptable. "But we would have to negotiate the size of the mosque," he added.

Asked why he thought Jeraise opposes the Islamic Movement on this matter, Abu Ahmad replied, "Because Jeraise wants our holy land to be subservient to his church."

Katsav has also asked the Antiquities Authority to analyze the remains found during excavation for the plaza to determine if they really are bones from ancient Moslem graves. Jeraise said that before he agrees to any compromise, he wants the results of this analysis to be made public "so the truth will come out."

The mayor maintains that Abu Ahmad and other local Moslem leaders invented the claims about ancient Moslem graves "strictly for purposes of incitement and political exploitation. And unfortunately, it worked," by affecting first the Nazareth municipal elections, then the upcoming national elections, and finally Israel's millennium celebrations.

"This little piece of land," said Jeraise, "is going to affect a lot of very big things."

As Moslem-Christian Tensions Escalate - Nazareth Mayor Attacked

Article by Haim Shapiro in the Jerusalem Post of Friday, June 11th, 1999

Moslem demonstrators in Nazareth yesterday attacked a car carrying Mayor Ramez Jeraise, injuring his driver.

The driver, Ne'emen Abu Ahmad, was hospitalized after being struck in the head, and three demonstrators were detained, police said.

The attack was part of continuing violence in the Galilee town, known as the home of Jesus, and could hurt plans to attract Christian pilgrims coming to mark the millennium.

At the heart of the conflict is an area near the Basilica of the Annunciation, where the municipality had planned to build a plaza to be the focus of millennium activities. However, over a year ago, Moslem activists set up a tent on the site, insisted that a mosque had once existed there, and a new mosque should be built.

The situation was exacerbated by the fact that in the last municipal elections Jeraise, a Christian, was re-elected, but a coalition representing the Islamic Movement, known as the United Arab List, won a majority of seats on the municipal council.

Since the election, the council has been convened only once. Interior Minister Eli Suissa appointed an inter-ministerial committee to deal with the problem, but as yet the committee has reached no conclusions.

Violence between Moslems and Christians erupted on both Christmas and Easter. On Wednesday, tensions rose again when several dozen Moslems staged a protest demonstration outside the municipality. A spokesman for the Nazareth Democratic Party, which Jeraise represents, said that the demonstrators harassed municipal workers as they left the building. The spokesman accused the police of not intervening at that time and during yesterday's attack.

Uri Mor, director of the Religious Affairs Ministry's department for Christian communities, said last night that as soon as he heard about the violence he called upon the police to intervene as soon as possible and avert bloodshed.

According to a government source, a senior Israeli official met last month with top-level officials in the Vatican. At that time, the source said, the officials asked that the government have the tent removed and see to it that a mosque is not built on the site.

Beit Jala Housing Project Exposes Identity Crisis

Article by Ben Lynfield in Jerusalem Post of Friday, June 11th, 1999

No one is willing to admit it, but Beit Jala, an ancient town of steeples and minarets wedged between the holy cities of Bethlehem and Jerusalem, appears to be in serious trouble.

Only the prospect of Palestinian Authority persuasion seemed yesterday to have much chance of bridging gaps between the mayor, Raji Zeidan, and nine of the 13 members of the city council who resigned last week, paralyzing the city government and raising questions about its ability to prepare for the Bethlehem 2000 celebrations next December.

As in other Christian-dominated or formerly Christian-dominated locales in the West Bank and inside Israel, Beit Jala's Christians are grappling with new demographic realities stemming from an influx of Moslems and an exodus by the younger generation to Latin American countries and the United States. Out of 13,500 residents, Beit Jala has 9-10,000 Christians according to Zeidan.

Bethlehem, once a Christian-dominated town, now has a clear Moslem majority, a fact that has not been lost on Beit Jala residents.

In large part, the councilors left because of their objections to plans for a new housing project that will house a large number of refugees and Moslems with roots outside the town. They say they were also uneasy with a more general non-enforcement of planning regulations. "My position is that there are some violations, as is the case everywhere, and that the municipality council must work steadily to solve the real problems of the city. It must be flexible and apply the spirit of the law, not the letter," Zeidan said.

All of those who quit the council are Christian, while those who stayed on, besides Zeidan, are Moslem. "I don't want to say {the objections to the project} were on the basis of racism," said Majed Yassiny, one of the city councilors who supports the project.

"We are all in the same homeland here. You can also find some Christians in the project. But there are some people in Beit Jala who think in a traditional and old-fashioned way that is not appropriate for this period. It's more of a social question than a religious one."

The project was to house mostly people linked to Fatah, according to Yassiny. Dimyan Alam, an engineer and leader of those who quit, said the plan called for it to be a six-story building of 70 units built in a "green area" that is, according to the town master plan, off-limits to construction.

"We have a master plan, we have to keep it and develop it, not to damage the {character} of the city by opening these areas," he said. And if green areas are to be opened up, Alam said, the tract for the housing project would be last on the list. The reason: It is at the lowest point in the city and is thus vulnerable to flooding.

But he also says he is concerned about the "special character" of the city. "I mean the standard of living and the different traditions. This is considered a highly civilized area, with respect to other areas in the PA."

Issa Allan, a city councilor who is staying on, says the flooding problem could be easily solved.

Palestinian "Policemen" Severed Electric Cables On A Street in the Christian Quarter

Article by Arnon Regular in the local "Kol Ha'ir" Jerusalem Weekly, June 11th, 1999 – (Translated from the Hebrew by Victor Mordecai)

Their intention evidently was to make identification more difficult in the event the (Israel) police was called in. Jerusalem Municipality lighting chief: Not the first time.

Members of one of the Palestinian security organizations who arrived this week (in Jerusalem) created a "black-out" in the Christian Quarter of the Old City. They cut the electric cables in the control box responsible for lighting in a number of Christian Quarter streets.

On the night between Monday and Tuesday, around midnight, two cars bearing Palestinian Authority license plates arrived at the parking area of the New Gate. Traveling in the two vehicles were eight men.

Two remained to guard the vehicles. The others accompanied by a local Old City resident and equipped with portable phones entered the alleyways. A few minutes later, the lights went out in a few streets in the quarter. An investigation by "Kol Ha'ir revealed that the cables in an electric box close to Casanova Street had been cut.

Evidently, the intention of the (Palestinian) security people was to make identification difficult in the event Israeli police was called in to the Christian Quarter. Two of the (Palestinian) security people entered a private home, but it is not known what they did there.

This is not the first time that unknown people have sabotaged the street lighting in that area. Jerusalem Municipality Lighting Department Head Yohanan Disney says that the manner in which the sabotage was carried out in the Old City has changed and that now well-trained professionals are carrying out this type of sabotage. Disney says that the Tuesday's sabotage was reported to the municipality and repaired. The police says it knows nothing about this event.

(In "Is Fanatic Islam a Global Threat?" I emphasized the orchestrated attack on the Christians of Bethlehem and their exodus over the last few years. Today, this scenario very sadly is repeating itself in Nazareth, Beit Jala, Ramallah, Beit Sahur, Turan and other cities were Arab Christians and Moslems have lived side-by-side for centuries. It seems the writing is on the wall for the Arab Christians unless there is a Christian Revival for Christian Survival in the Holy Land! — Victor Mordecai)

The following article by Efraim Inbar in the Jerusalem Post of March 8th, 1999 has really nothing to do with harassment or persecution of the Christians in the Holy Land. But I thought to present this article as part of this book to show a reality facing both Jews and Christians in Israel. Today there are roughly five million Jews and Christians living under the flag and sovereignty of Israel. Compared to this, there are over one million Moslem Israeli Arabs and about 2.5 million Palestinians in Judea, Samaria and Gaza. This unhealthy balance is one of the reasons why many Jews in Israel want to see a Palestinian state or entity so that the 2.5 million Palestinians, most of them Moslems, will not be counted anymore as being under Israeli sovereignty and therefore part of the final demographic reality. According to some estimates, within 20 to 30 years, the total number of Moslem Arabs will be greater than the total number of Jews and Christians under the Holy Land totality. This would present Israel with the threat of Islamic takeover or apartheid, South African style. Neither of these alternatives can be acceptable to the Jewish State.

The Risk of Open Borders
by Efraim Inbar

Israelis have always dreamed of open borders with their neighbors. For us, this has always meant being able to travel freely to eat humous in Damascus or to shop in Beirut. After being able to open an embassy in an Arab capital, this has been the litmus test for the type of peace we desire.

In contrast to Israel's territorial demands, the condition of free movement of people and goods across borders has the full support of the US, which accepts this Israeli interpretation of the quality of peace it expects in exchange for conquered territories. Free trade and open borders between states have always been the liberal recipe for prosperity and peace.

It is high time we reconsidered this emphasis on the free flow of people and goods, particularly if the differences in economic performance between us and our neighbors continues to grow.

Numbers are often boring, but instructive. The statistics provided by the London-based International Institute for Strategic Studies show that the disparity in the wealth of the average resident of Israel compared to his neighbors is very great. While the annual GNP per capita in Israel in 1997 was $17,800, the respective figures for Egypt, Jordan, Lebanon, the Palestinian Authority and Syria were: $4,400; $4,700; $4,800; $1,600; and $6,700.

The Israeli standard of living is thus nearly three to four times higher than that of our neighboring states and 10 times higher than that of the Palestinians.

History has shown that an affluent country surrounded by poor neighbors generally elicits one of two responses from its destitute environment: immigration or conquest.

Rome was conquered by much poorer hordes of barbarians. The Rome of today, the United States struggles unsuccessfully to stop illegal immigrants coming in from Mexico. Prosperous contemporary Europe is inundated by waves of illegal immigrants from Third World countries. Germany alone has over five million foreigners on its soil.

Israel has gradually become a Western affluent society, which serves as a magnet for people trying to improve their economic lot. One clear reason for the Jewish immigration from countries of the former Soviet Union was the high standard of living Israel was offering.

Israel's economy has also attracted, however, at least 250,000 foreign workers, from Romania, Thailand, Turkey and Black Africa, ready to do the menial jobs Israelis are unwilling to take. Some of them have established families here, or brought their families from their home countries. The children of foreign workers constitute 40 percent of the pupils in some schools in south Tel-Aviv.

Israel's workforce also includes tens of thousands of Palestinians, most of whom go back to their homes every day after working hours. Some, though, do not. There is increasing political pressure to allow Jordanian workers to commute to work in Israel. Jordan justly wants to show its population some peace dividends.

Egypt could also become a source of cheap labor for the Israeli economy. There are already several thousand illegal Egyptian workers in our midst. Fortunately, there is a desert between Israel and the overpopulated Nile delta, or we would have long ago seen a stream of Egyptians trying to cross the border to find work in Israel.

Similarly, the state of war between Israel and Syria spares the Jewish state from an influx of Syrian workers trying to make a living in the Galilee. It should be noted that there are about one million Syrian workers in Lebanon. Many of them will probably stay, facilitating Syria's conquest of Lebanon.

In contrast to countries such as the US or Germany, Israel does not have the demographic critical mass to withstand the pressures of an internationally mobile manpower market. Our porous borders could prove to be an existential threat, because they could challenge the state's Jewish majority by mere immigration. Israel cannot afford to have too many foreign workers because as history shows, many of them stay for good.

It is easier to close the borders to overseas job hunters than to our immediate neighbors, and while the responsibility for the economic conditions among our neighbors is with the Arab leaders, Israel has a clear interest in not having its neighbors too hungry.

Simply put, such neighbors are dangerous. Our homes are already being burglarized and our cars stolen as a result of the Green Line's permeability. This is an issue of internal security, which might be transformed into a severe external security challenge if not dealt with adequately.

Thus, our traditional demand for open borders with our neighbors is not necessarily in Israel's interest.

Victor Mordecai comments:

1. At the beginning of this book, I mentioned that there are two systems - the system of the "haves" who follow God's system and the other - that of the "have-nots" - those who follow anti-God systems. The countries immediately surrounding Israel are Islamic anti-God systems. This explains the differential in GNP per capita. In the above articles about Nazareth and Beit Jala, we read about the frustration of the growing Moslem population with the richer Christians who have fewer children. This helps to explain why since the beginning of this century, the percentage of Christians in the Middle East has dropped from 25% to 2%. The Christians fled the growing and

threatening Islamic numbers around and opted to emigrate to America or Europe.

2. Mark Twain once visited the Holy Land in the late 1800's and saw a stark lunarscape, devoid virtually of any trees or human population. In his book about that visit, Mark Twain said that if this were the "Promised Land" he would be very happy that this land not be promised to him. Indeed, the Holy Land was destroyed by centuries of Islamic misrule and abuse. It was only after the Jewish people started to return in increasing numbers to the Land of Israel in the late 1800's that the desert was planted with trees, the malarial swamps were drained and a forbidding hell was turned into a Garden of Eden. At the same time, there was a parallel immigration to the Land of Israel by Arab laborers from Lebanon, Syria, Jordan, Saudi Arabia, Egypt and even the Sudan. There never was a Palestinian people. The so-called Palestinians are descendants of Muslim immigrants to Israel who wanted to live off the plenty and prosperity the Jews were bringing, but not to allow for an infidel Jewish State. This explains the Palestinian and pan-Arab, pan-Islamic rejection of the creation of Jewish and Arab states in the Holy Land in 1947 and the resulting Palestinian refugee problem. While the Jews naturally took in their Jewish brethren expelled from Islamic countries, the Moslems naturally refused to do anything for their Palestinian brethren fleeing at the behest of the Arab High Command promising them Jewish homes and properties as loot after the Jews were driven into the sea. Most Palestinian refugees were holed up in refugee camps in order to perpetuate the problem.

3. As Jews and Christians flee the majorities created by higher Islamic birthrates, the country collapses back into the anti-God "have-not" system, a black hole, a Catch-22. There is no democracy in Islam. There is no Islamic country that has any industry to speak of other than petroleum, which is a gift from God squandered by those who believe in Allah, the moon god, the war god.

4. Now, thanks to NATO, the world has not only Islamic Albania in Europe. It now has Islamic Bosnia and Islamic Kosovo. Sit back and "enjoy" or rather squirm when you see the results of the economic and political situation as it develops in

the Balkans. The same applies to the Palestinian Autonomy. Try to find a flowering economy under Arafat and his henchmen and all you will find is centralized economic control with guess who pulling the strings. There can be no economic improvement in the lot of the Palestinians under the PA's misrule.

Now, from the Holy Land, one of the smallest pieces of real estate in the world, I would like to present some more articles from the Jerusalem Post regarding the world's most populous Islamic country, Indonesia, and review briefly the status of Christians there.

Tortured Bodies Found in Indonesia's Ambon

Article on page 7 of the Jerusalem Post of March 3rd, 1999

Ambon (Reuters) - Two stabbed and tortured bodies were found yesterday in Indonesia's scarred island of Ambon, which remained tense after two days of bloody religious clashes, police said.

The bodies of a man and woman, both Christians, were found on in Air Kuning, some 10 km. West of Ambon City.

It brings the number of dead in violence in the area to 12 since Sunday. Clashes between Moslems and Christians have hit the eastern island for weeks.

There were unconfirmed reports that a third body, a man, had also been found nearby.

One Dead in Ambon Clash, Dozens Arrested

Article on page 5 of the Jerusalem Post of Sunday, March 14, 1999

Ambon, Indonesia (Reuters) - One Christian died yesterday during fighting involving hundreds of people in the capital of the violence-torn Indonesian island of Ambon, witnesses and church sources said.

In a separate incident, police said they had arrested 37 Moslem youths who were found with weapons and plans for a Saturday night attack on Christian refugees.

Fighting broke out in two outlying areas of Ambon city in the morning, witnesses said. In the Batu Merah area, a crowd of Moslems stabbed and killed a Christian, Christian sources said.

Fighting was also reported in the Benteng area of the city, where a peace agreement between local Christians and Moslems had just been signed. Few other details were immediately available.

60 Die In Indonesian Religious Violence

Article from Jerusalem Post of April 6th, 1999

Jakarta (AP) - The number of people killed amid an outbreak of religious violence on two remote islands in eastern Indonesia rose yesterday to 60 after more victims' bodies were found in burned-out houses.

The official Antara news agency quoted local military sources as saying 20 badly charred corpses were recovered yesterday in Larat, a village on Kai Besar Island in Maluku province, once known as the Spice Islands.

More than 250 people have been killed and hundreds of houses and buildings burned in Maluku since bloody clashes first erupted between Christians and Moslems in January.

Fighting erupted on Dula Island in the Kai Islands group on Wednesday. The bloodshed spread to neighboring Kai Besar Island on Friday. Antara quoted witnesses as saying the bodies had been burned beyond recognition.

But the local military chief, Lt. Col. Ery Susanto, said the situation in Larat was under control yesterday.

"I have instructed military personnel posted in the village to evacuate and bury those bodies," Susanto was quoted as saying by Antara.

Two Christians were killed by Moslems in a separate clash on Sunday in Tual, the capital of Southeast Maluku on Dula Island, about 2,800 kilometers east of Jakarta.

Susanto said some villagers feared further outbreaks of violence and had armed themselves with swords, knives and other weapons despite calls for peace by officials.

He said the military wanted villagers to stay in their homes and not to attempt to leave their islands, adding that the navy would send several warships to the region to avert an exodus.

Boats that try to take people away would be stopped, Susanto said.

More than 13,000 people have already fled their homes for the shelter in government and military installations in Tual.

Antara said at least 200 children among the refugees there were suffering from contagious diseases, including diarrhea.

Though nearly 90 percent of Indonesia's 210 million people are Moslems, Maluku has a large Christian population.

The violence in Maluku comes amid Indonesia's worst economic crisis in decades as well as political uncertainty that has followed the resignation of authoritarian president Suharto last May. Rioting and lawlessness have hit many parts of Indonesia since Suharto stepped down after 32 years in power.

Last month more than 200 people were killed in ethnic fighting on the island of Borneo.

Antara reported that fresh violence had broken out there on Sunday and continued into yesterday in the worst hit district of Sambas.

Some 17 houses were set on fire, but there was no immediate report on casualties.

Indonesia Troops Kill Several in East Timor

Article from Jeruaslem Post of Sunday, April 18th, 1999

Dili, East Timor (Reuters) - Several people died on Saturday when Indonesian troops opened fire on a house sheltering dozens of East Timorese, according to a prominent campaigner for the territory's independence.

The report of the shooting came after a pro-Jakarta militia leader told a rally that East Timor should be cleansed of pro-Independence (Christian) groups. Militiamen went on a rampage after the rally, burning cars and houses, witnesses said.

Leading pro-independence activist Manuel Carascalao told Reuters his teenage son and several other people were killed when his house was attacked,

"My son was killed in the attack on my house and I believe that there are several others who were killed in the incident," he said by telephone from Dili.

"I don't know where my son is, but all I know is that he has been killed by the (Indonesian) troops," Carascalao added.

Carascalao, the brother of a former Jakarta-appointed governor in the territory, said that at the time of the attack around 100 people were in the house, most of who had sought refuge there.

Police and military in the area were not available for immediate comment but the Indonesian military commander for East Timor, Colonel Tono Suratman, later inspected the house with officials from the International Committee of the Red Cross, witnesses said.

Saturday's unrest started with a rally of more than 1,000 pro-Jakarta militiamen brandishing rifles and machetes in front of the Jakarta-appointed governor's office.

Militia commander Eurico Gutteres told his followers to clear the territory of groups supporting independence.

"Starting today, I command all pro-integration militias to conduct a cleansing of all those who betrayed integration. Capture and kill if you need," he said.

The mob also attacked the office of the local newspaper in East Timor and ransacked the place and other buildings around the small town. Police and soldiers appeared to make no effort to stop the militiamen as they rampaged through the streets.

Many of the militiamen wore headbands in red and white - the colors of the Indonesian flag.

Indonesian loyalists have stepped up their campaign of attacks and public rallies as Indonesia and Portugal discuss an East Timor ballot on whether the former Portuguese colony wants independence or more autonomy within Indonesia.

Guerrillas fighting for independence have also stepped up their activities, with several attacks in the past few days after months of silence.

Detained guerrilla leader Xanana Gusmao has called on his supporters to take up arms in the face of increasing action by the pro-Jakarta militias.

But his call has also sparked fears that United Nations-brokered efforts by Jakarta and Lisbon to thrash out a peaceful solution to the East Timor problem could fail.

Foreign ministers from the two countries are due to meet in New York next week. They are expected to strike an agreement on holding a vote on autonomy or independence.

Indonesia invaded East Timor in 1975 and annexed it the following year in a move not recognized by the United Nations.

More than 200,000 East Timorese - about a quarter of the population - have died in the fighting and through starvation and disease.

East Timorese Retrieve Bodies after New Attacks

Article on page 5 of the Jerusalem Post of April 25th, 1999

Dili, East Timor (Reuters) - East Timorese villagers pulled rotting corpses from the ocean yesterday after new attacks by pro-Jakarta militia, despite a UN-brokered deal that could lead to the territory's independence.

Church and human rights workers said they fear the final death toll from last week's bloodletting may top 100.

They could not say how many bodies were retrieved from southern Suai, about 200 km southwest of Dili. At least eight victims of attacks by the militia fighting for continued Indonesian rule had previously been identified.

"The number may be more than 100 dead because the attacks were scattered over several districts and reports are still coming in," a Dili-based human rights worker, who asked not to be identified, told Reuters.

"The situation in Suai is very, very tense," he added, saying refugees had sheltered in a church.

"About 1,300 refugees have been asked to leave the church because they fear an attack like in Liquisa or Dili," he said, referring to earlier attacks this month in which up to 50 may have died.

"Along the sea, they have thrown in bodies and some have washed up on the beach. Some are already smelly, but there are also fresh bodies there," he said.

He said there was no detailed body count yet because the victims were killed in sporadic attacks since Monday in several areas around Suai.

A local priest, Father Hilario, said Friday he feared last week's death toll may top 100 and that the eight identified victims had been shot or stabbed.

Around 30 people died in an earlier militia rampage last weekend.

Military and police officials were unavailable for comment yesterday. But one military official in Dili and an official at the hospital in Suai said Friday there were no deaths.

As tensions increase and some pro-independence leaders go into hiding, former Jakarta-appointed governor Mario Carrascalao, who has campaigned for an independence vote, said East Timorese mercenaries have been hired to kill him.

Carrascalao, appealing for official protection, said he has received death threats and is taking his family to Portugal for their safety, but said he will return to his Jakarta home.

Loyalist militias stepped up their bloody anti-independence campaign after Indonesian President B.J. Habibie reversed a 23 year policy in January and said Jakarta may let East Timor go it alone if it rejected an offer of enhanced autonomy.

Dili-based human rights groups say up to 90 people died in attacks by pro-Jakarta militia and the Indonesian armed forces in the first three months of 1999.

The warring factions signed a peace pact Wednesday, but the militias continue to carry guns, control some roads and effectively seal Dili off each night with roadblocks.

Jakarta and Lisbon Friday completed an agreement paving the way for a UN-organized July ballot on independence in July or August.

The agreement will be signed on May 5 to give Jakarta more time to approve new sections in the accord on security and how the vote will be conducted.

New Religious Riot Breaks Out in Indonesia

Article on page 5 of the Jerusalem Post of Sunday, April 25th, 1999

Tual, Indonesia (AP) - Sectarian violence erupted for a second day yesterday in eastern Indonesia, where witnesses said Moslems hurled homemade bombs at Christians. The number of dead and injured was unclear. The attack occurred in Uun, a hillside village on the outskirts of Tual, the main town on the remote Kai Besar Island, witnesses said. One person who claimed to be at the scene said "dozens" of people were killed. Lt. Col. Simson Munthe, chief of the local police, confirmed the violence but said, "only a small number of people were shot dead by security forces." More than 300 people have died in fighting in Maluku province this year. Dozens of churches and mosques have been burned.

(Victor Mordecai comments: It is really tragic that Yugoslav President Slobodan Milosevic is such a war criminal. Yugoslavia is responsible for the deaths of 10,000 Albanian Kosovars in a war of self-defense and maintenance of sovereignty. Yet in the above articles we see an ongoing war in Indonesia with over 200,000 Christians slaughtered by Moslems, but the so-called "liberal" western leaders remain strangely silent. Could it be because Indonesia is part of the petroleum exporting nations' cartel?)

In neighboring Philippines, there is also a war between Christians and Moslems. The following are a couple of articles I thought to use in "Is Fanatic Islam a Global Threat?" but for lack of time and space, I postponed using these articles.

Philippines, Moslem Rebels Make Peace

Article by Claro Cortes of AP in the Jerusalem Post of September 3rd, 1996

Supporters and opponents of a peace settlement with Moslem rebels demonstrated yesterday as negotiators signed a final agreement ending a 26-year rebellion that cost more than 120,000 lives.

The government has agreed in the pact to provide increased autonomy to Moslem areas in the southern Philippines, while the rebels dropped their demand for a separate Moslem state.

Outside Manila's Malacanang presidential palace, several thousand Christian and Moslem supporters of the agreement released yellow and blue balloons and honked car horns to celebrate as the pact was signed.

But in southern Iligan City, the city government flew flags at half-mast and about 4,000 city employees and others attended a rally against the agreement.

"Here in Iligan there is only worry and cries of sadness, not of joy," said city councilor Lawrence Cruz. The agreement, he said, "is driving a wedge between the Christians and Moslems."

And in Zamboanga City, a new militant Christian group declared war against supporters of the agreement. The group, the Mindanao Christian Unified Command, is being blamed for three small explosions last Friday.

Many Christians living in the southern Philippines fear the pact gives too much power to the rebels.

But during yesterday's signing ceremony inside the palace, both sides praised the agreement.

"This could mean the end of scourge and darkness for our people," said rebel chief Nur Misuari.

Misuari, a quiet-spoken, bearded former university professor, wore a dark suit and fez to the ceremony instead of his former battle fatigues.

More than 1,500 government and rebel officials - some in colorful traditional dress - and representatives of Moslem nations watched Misuari and chief government negotiator Manuel Yan sign the agreement, finalized just last week.

The pact is a major achievement for President Fidel Ramos, who has sought since taking office four years ago to settle three separate insurgencies - by Moslem rebels, Communists and right-wing soldiers - that have destabilized the nation and impeded economic growth.

Although two smaller Moslem rebel groups still reject the peace pact, the acceptance by Misuari's Moro National Liberation Front means that Ramos' administration has now largely settled two of the three rebellions.

Military officers who led a series of coup attempts against Ramos' predecessor, Corazon Aquino, have been granted amnesty and some have even become senators, but talks with divided Communist rebels still have not succeeded.

Ramos warned that the government must now focus on eliminating poverty and injustice in the south, one of the Philippines poorest yet resource-rich regions.

"The root causes of conflict will not go away just because we have signed this agreement," he said. "Never again must Filipinos be so desperate as to take up arms against one another."

Under the agreement, the MNLF will control a new peace council that will oversee economic development projects in 14 impoverished southern provinces for three years.

Negotiators believe this will give the rebels a chance to demonstrate their leadership and lessen the war's fears and hatred.

Then in 1999, a plebiscite will be held to determine which of the provinces wish to join a new autonomous government.

The rebels consider the 14 provinces their Moslem homeland, but generations of Christian settlers have come to dominate the region. Tens of thousands of Christians have demonstrated in recent weeks against the pact.

Filipino Militia Kills 33 Moslem Guerrillas Last Week

Article from page 4 of the Jerusalem Post of Sunday October 27, 1996

Zamboanga, Philippines (AP) - At least 33 Muslim rebels have been killed in several days of fighting on a southern Philippine island despite a government cease-fire offer, the military said Friday.

Air Force planes bombed and fired rockets Friday at guerrilla positions on the mountains around Tipo-Tipo town in Basilan province, about 900 km (560 miles) south of Manila.

The fighting flared up earlier this week when Moro Islamic Liberation Front guerrillas ambushed an army patrol, wounding five soldiers. Six more soldiers were injured in the fighting that followed.

The MILF is one of several Muslim rebel splinter groups still fighting the government after the larger Moro National Liberation Front signed a peace agreement lat month, ending a quarter-century rebellion that killed more than 120,000 people in the southern Philippines.

Tipo-Tipo town council member Alton Angeles appealed for relief supplies for at least 600 people who fled to the town center from their remote villages to avoid the crossfire.

In addition to Christian-Muslim conflicts, there is a continuing Hindu-Muslim struggle for control of the provinces of Jammu and Kashmir.

The following are articles updating information which already appeared in "Is Fanatic Islam a Global Threat?"

Kashmir Gets Scarier

Article by Stephen Kinzer in the Sunday New York Times of June 20, 1999

Srinagar, Kashmir – High in the forbidding Himalayan foothills north of here, the half-century-old struggle for control of Kashmir is entering a new and unpredictable phase. Islamic fighters have crossed the line that divides the state between zones of Indian and Pakistani control, and the Indian Army is waging a bloody campaign to drive them back. It is the latest battle in a conflict that has taken tens of thousands of lives over the last decade.

In the wake of the Kosovo campaign, awareness is growing in Washington and other capitals that the world pays a high price for waiting too long to address growing crises. The one in Kashmir is among the most combustible, and the fact that both contending nations are armed with nuclear weapons lends it an apocalyptic urgency. It is now drawing more serious attention than at any time since it started.

When President Clinton telephoned the Prime Ministers of India and Pakistan last week to urge them to resolve this crisis, he was stepping gingerly, and on territory where few outsiders have dared to tread at all. His message was vague and tentative, but in suggesting that Pakistan use its influence to pull the insurgents out of Indian territory, he was at least signaling the world's growing fear that this obscure conflict could spiral out of control.

"We're facing a small war, but it can escalate," one of Kashmir's wise men, Sufi Ghulan Mohammed, editor of the Urdu-language Srinagar Times, said last week. "Escalation means devastation. It does not have to be planned. Anything can happen at any time.

The Kashmir conflict overlaid with religious passion as well as chauvinistic competition is perhaps even more complex than those that have shaken the Balkans. Kashmir is about 75 percent Muslim, but when India and Pakistan were created in 1947, the maharajah, a Hindu, chose to lead it into Hindu-dominated India rather than Islamic Pakistan. He felt that the mixed society he ruled would fare better in an avowedly secular state than one devoted to a single religion.

Pakistan has never accepted Kashmir's accession to India, and has waged two wars to seize it. The last one, in 1971, ended with a cease-fire that left two-thirds of the state in India and the rest in Pakistan.

One reason the conflict is so difficult to solve is that in different ways, Kashmir is central to the national ideals of both India and Pakistan. Indian leaders fear that losing Kashmir would set off a wave of separatist movements in other Indian states, and implicitly accept the failure of the premise on which India is built: that it can embrace peoples of many different religions.

Pakistan, in contrast, was built on the idea that all Muslims on the sub-continent should live in their own state. Allowing all or part of Kashmir to remain under Indian rule contradicts that.

Some powerful Pakistanis believe that Kashmir represents the unfinished agenda of the 1947 partition. Others see war here as a way to punish India for its support of Pakistani rebels who succeeded in separating Bangladesh from Pakistan in 1971. But the real fire behind the current conflict is the desire of Islamic militants to wrest control of what they consider a Muslim land from the control of infidels. Many of them fought in Afghanistan; some are loyal to the anti-Western Muslim fundamentalist Osama bin Laden.

Over the years Pakistan has sought to internationalize the issue by bringing it before the United Nations and other bodies. India opposes all such efforts, and insists that the questions be resolved only by the two nations. But President Clinton's telephone calls last week, along with expected discussions of the problem at this weekend's meeting of leaders of the biggest industrialized countries in Germany, suggest that India may now have to accept the world's growing concern.

In the wake of the holocaust in Rwanda and successive catastrophes in the former Yugoslavia, many voices are being raised in favor of intervening before future crises around the globe reach the point of explosion. There is still no consensus on how, when or where to act, and much fear about the consequences of aggressive intervention. But few international summits are likely to pass now without discussion of the possibility of assertive action in places like Kashmir.

Kashmir is a good place to start because it reflects not only how dangerous obscure wars can become but also how difficult it is to resolve them. Many people in the Indian-held section are highly suspicious of Pakistan, which is in even worse social, economic and political shape than India, and where religious fundamentalism is on the rise. But they have no love for the Indian security forces, which human rights groups say regularly ransack and burn villages, torture prisoners and assassinate suspected militants.

Over the years, some Indian leaders have suggested that the solution lies in giving the province what Prime Minister Narasimha Rao in 1995 called "anything short of independence" and what Prime Minister Deve Gowda a year later called "maximum autonomy." That, however, is anathema to much of the Indian establishment, which fears a precedent for splintering India itself.

Every proposed solution, in fact, is fraught with danger. To reach a lasting peace, all three sides would have to make historic compromises involving their basic principles.

In addition to the West, China, which borders Kashmir and faces a rising Islamic movement in its own western provinces, is increasingly worried and increasingly ready to apply pressure for a solution. But if outside powers are to break this deadlock, they need strong partners in both India and Pakistan, leaders who can break with the past and persuade their peoples to do so too. No such leaders are on the horizon.

Two Indian Warplanes Lost Over Pakistan's Part of Kashmir

Excerpts from article by Barry Bearak in New York Times of Friday, May 28, 1999

New Delhi, May 27th – Two Indian fighter jets were lost in combat today on the Pakistani side of the cease-fire line in troubled Kashmir, worsening the confrontation between the subcontinent's two nuclear-armed rivals.

Both aircraft had been taking part in a second day of Indian rocket attacks against Islamic guerrillas who have seized mountaintop positions a few miles inside Indian territory. These Himalayan perches overlook supply routes that extend from the Kashmir Valley to an important Indian military base in Ladakh.

Militant separatists challenge Indian's control. India routinely insists that Pakistan, which is predominantly Muslim, finances and arms these guerrillas, a charge that Pakistan invariably denies.

There are many unanswered questions about the 500 to 600 militants who have established well-fortified positions in northern Kashmir's snow-capped, oxygen-thin peaks. These guerrillas are equipped with snowmobiles and heavy artillery, the Indians say, and they are being re-supplied by helicopter.

To India, the guerrillas' ability to sustain themselves in some of the world's least hospitable terrains proves the coordinating hand of the Pakistani armed forces. In fact, the Indians charge that Pakistani soldiers are fighting alongside guerrillas predominantly from Afghanistan.

On this score, many Western experts agree with the Indians. It seems most likely, they say, that the militants are sponsored by Pakistan, or perhaps even by one of Pakistan's intelligence agencies operating without Government knowledge.

Selig Harrison, a South Asia expert with the 20th Century Fund, said that while the Islamic militants have not been successful in Pakistan's elections, they have come to wield influence in the intelligence agencies. And on of those agencies, he said, could not be involved in supporting the large guerrilla presence in the remote mountains.

(Victor Mordecai comments: In "Is Fanatic Islam a Global Threat?" I reviewed three different newspaper articles regarding Islamic irredentism in western China. Pakistan figures as one of the supporters of these Islamic warrior groups. Similarly, in the assassination of moderate Muslim cleric Rashad Khalifa in Tucson, Arizona on January 30th, 1990, the Muslim assassins were known to have visited Pakistan. Finally, Pakistan and the Afghani Taliban are working closely together to destabilize not only India and China, but even Iran and the former Soviet republics as well. The following are articles regarding the never-ending civil war in Afghanistan as well as terrorism in Uzebekistan.)

US Negotiator Briefs India on Talks with Pakistan

Article on page 5 of the Jerusalem Post of June 28th, 1999

Dras, India (AP) - An American envoy yesterday briefed India on talks with Pakistan aimed at defusing the seven-week crisis in northern Kashmir, as India refused to talk to Pakistan until armed intruders leave Indian territory.

Army Chief of Staff General V.P. Malik flew to the northern battle zone to consult with his commanders, while troops inched up a crucial mountain peak overlooking the highway which is India's only supply line in the region.

The air force bombed mountaintop positions around the clock for the past two days, a Defense Ministry spokesman said.

The air force has been in action for the past month, in its first combat missions since the 1971 war with Pakistan.

India accuses Pakistan of sending hundreds of its soldiers and Islamic guerrillas to seize mountain positions in the Kargil region of Indian-held Kashmir. On Saturday, Pakistan's army chief appeared to admit for the first time his troops were involved when he said they would not be withdrawn unilaterally.

US Deputy Assistant Secretary of State Gibson Lanpher briefed Indian officials on talks held in Pakistan last week by Marine Corps Gen. Anthony Zinni, chief of the US Central Command.

Zinni reportedly carried a message to Islamabad from President Bill Clinton, urging Pakistan to withdraw its forces.

"I have brought no proposals," Lanpher told Indian reporters who asked if Washington had suggested ways to deescalate the tension. He said Zinni did not discuss the possibility of safe corridor for the fighters in his talks with Pakistan, as has been speculated in the Indian media.

Afghan Opposition Says Taliban Preparing For War

The following appeared on page 7 of the Jerusalem Post of April 15th, 1999

Islamabad, Pakistan (AP) – Afghanistan's ruling Taliban religious army, with help from neighboring Pakistan, is preparing for an all-out war, the country's beleaguered opposition claimed yesterday. In a letter to UN Secretary-General Kofi Annan, Afghanistan's northern-based opponents accused Pakistan of sending massive shipments of weapons and paramilitary soldiers to help the Taliban.

Pakistan routinely denies giving any kind of assistance to the Taliban army, which rules 90 percent of Afghanistan with strict Islamic laws. But Pakistan is sympathetic to the Taliban and is one of only three countries to give it official recognition.

Taliban Jets Bomb Opposition In Afghanistan

The following appeared on page 5 of the Jerusalem Post of April 25th, 1999.

Kabul (AP) Taliban fighter jets pounded opposition positions Saturday in Afghanistan's central Bamiyan province to try to recapture the provincial capital, an opposition spokesman said.

"Their fighter planes bombarded us all day long," said Mohammed Jawari, a spokesman for the opposition Shi'ite Moslem group, Hezb-e-Wahadat. The Taliban had not sent in ground troops. In its first significant victory in more than a year, the opposition routed the Taliban from Bamiyan last Wednesday. Since then, there have been reports the Taliban are regrouping and will launch an offensive within days to recapture Bamiyan, 180 miles northwest of the capital, Kabul. In a string of victories, the Taliban, or the students of Islam, captured Bamiyan last year, ejecting the Hezb-e-Wahadat.

Uzebekistan President Escapes Attack

Article by Timofei Zhukov in Jerusalem Post of Wednesday, February 17th, 1999.

Tashkent, Uzbekistan (AP) – A bomb ripped through Uzbekistan's government headquarters yesterday, followed by a shoot-out and several other explosions aimed at killing President Islam Karimov.

At least nine people were killed and dozens injured in six nearly simultaneous explosions, five of them car bombs, the government said.

Karimov appeared on state-controlled television shortly after the blasts and said they were an attempt to assassinate him. The authoritarian president had been expected at the government headquarters when the bombs went off, but changed his plans at the last minute and was not present, the Interfax news agency said.

The blasts took place before a scheduled cabinet meeting. No one immediately claimed responsibility for the attack.

"The task of these people was to spoil our present lives, to mislead the people, to scare the people," Karimov said. "Let them know that we have the strength and trust that we've chosen the right path. No force will ever make us change the course."

Karimov has led Uzbekistan since it gained independence in 1991, and yesterday's attack was one of the worst outbreaks of violence during his tenure.

Karimov's government maintains tight security even during times of calm, and it stepped up its efforts immediately following the blast.

The bombed buildings were cordoned off. Roadblocks were set up and traffic was re-routed. Planes, trains and buses were not allowed to travel in the hours immediately after the attack.

The first bomb went off in the lobby of the government headquarters in Tashkent. Shortly afterward, a car broke through a police cordon set around the site of the blast, prompting security guards to open fire. Two attackers were killed in a shoot-out, according to a policeman.

The car itself then exploded, and then four more cars exploded around the city.

"By all appearances it was a terrorist act, because the cars all blew up at the same time," the Emergency Situations Committee said in a statement.

Among the sites targeted in the blasts were the Interior Affairs Ministry, the National Bank, and a building that housed several embassies.

The blast at the National Bank damaged several of the building's 22 stories, and police reported numerous injuries and possible deaths.

Russian President Boris Yeltsin condemned the attack in a statement issued in Moscow, calling it a "cynical terrorist act."

Karimov has frequently cracked down on political opponents and has drawn criticism from international human rights groups.

There has been sporadic unrest in Uzbekistan in recent years, but Karimov is considered to have a firm grip on power.

Karimov argues that his tough policies have maintained stability in Uzbekistan and prevented any spillover of the turmoil that has wracked the Central Asian nations of Afghanistan and Tajikistan.

Uzbekistan Asks Israel's Help Against Hizbullah

Article taken from page 2 of the Jerusalem Post of Thursday, February 18th, 1999 – by Danna Harman

Uzbeki President Islam Karimov, who barely escaped an attack on his life Tuesday, said yesterday he believed he was targeted by a Hizbullah group.

Speaking by phone to Industry and Trade Minister Natan Sharansky, Karimov said that Hizbullah offshoots have penetrated the former Soviet Union and were sprouting up in Uzbekistan as well. Karimov, who has spoken out strongly against fundamentalism in the past, told Sharansky that Israel and Uzbekistan must coordinate efforts against such terror attacks.

Police Identify Suspects in Uzbek Explosion

Article appearing on page 7 of the Jerusalem Post of Friday, February 19, 1999

Tashkent, Uzbekistan (AP) - The Uzbek police appealed over state television yesterday, for help in finding a married couple it identified as suspects in a series of car bombs that killed 14 people earlier this week.

Television transmitted pictures of Ulugbek and Dildora Babadzhanov, and said they were from the Fergana Valley, an Uzbek region with a strong Islamic tradition.

No one has claimed responsibility for the six car bombs, which exploded within minutes of one another outside government buildings Tuesday, but Islamic militants have come under suspicion. Television said the man and woman being sought were born in 1971 and 1977, respectively.

(Victor Mordecai comments: According to CNN World Report, over twenty suspects were in the process of being tried for these bombings as of June 1999 during the writing of this book.)

As I mentioned earlier in this book, I had the opportunity in June 1994 to visit Russia. and Radio Moscow. My host, Oleg Gribkov, provided me with his testimony about the Islamic soldiers from Bosnia, Albania and Kosovo who participated in Hitler's war on Russia. But I also provided him with a testimony, or prediction, rather, that not only was the West not any more the enemy of Russia or vice versa, but the exact opposite was true. Russia was no longer Communist Russia, but Christian Russia, part of the Judeo-Christian West. I told him that Russia would be targeted as the rest of Europe, America and Israel as the enemy of Islam. He brushed off my warnings and, as a good, old, loyal Communist that he was stressed the "fraternity of all nations" as preached by Communist ideology. I warned him, "Watch out! You will have your Chechnya, Bosnia and Kosovo to deal with as well as other Islamic problems throughout the rest of Russia where there are Islamic population concentrations.

At the end of our visit, when I told him I am a Jew who warns the Christians in their churches about what is about to come up against them, he finally asked me, "Would you come to Russia to speak in our churches as well?"

Russia Seeks Clues in Market Bombing

Article by Peter Henderson in Jerusalem Post of Sunday, March 21st, 1999

Moscow (Reuters) - The Russian government said yesterday a market bombing which killed more than 50 could be the work of religious extremists while newspapers looked for clues in the battle for power in neighboring Chechnya.

Officials revised downwards the death toll from Friday's blast, saying 51 were killed when the blast tore through the main market in Vladikavkaz, about 50 km from Russia's breakaway republic of Chechnya. Previously police had estimated the number of dead at 61.

"World analogies, as a rule, indicated that representatives of religious fanatics are often responsible for such acts," Interior Minister Serge Stepashin told Russian television from Vladikavkaz in volatile southern Russia.

He said bomb fragments would be examined in Moscow laboratories for clues to the bomb's origin.

The Emergencies Ministry and a spokesman for the head of Northern Ossetia region, of which Vladikavkaz is the capital, agreed on the death toll and said 154 had been injured, of whom 82 were in hospital.

The Kremlin announced that today would be a national day of mourning for victims of the bombing and of a fire in another region that killed more than 20 people earlier in the week.

Police made composite images, based on witnesses' accounts, of two suspects who deposited a bag in the market and left minutes before the explosion, Lev Dzugayev, press secretary for regional government head Alexander Dzasokhov, told Reuters.

He said no opposition group in the region was capable of such an act. "It must be outside forces," he said by telephone from the region.

The explosion occurred in the area of the crowded market where potatoes were sold, the Emergency Ministry said.

Television pictures showed bloodstained wreckage of market stalls and bodies amid heaps of potatoes and clothing.

Officials have said the bomb may have been meant to undermine regional political stability and the federal government's reputation.

The newspaper Kommersant Daily said violence had spilled out of Chechnya as the war torn republic tried to make a collective choice on its future between religious and secular leaders.

Chechen President Aslan Maskhadov is expected to visit Moscow for talks in the coming days. Kommersant said the opposition might be eager to foment a conflict between neighboring regions to keep Russia occupied.

Dzugayev said the federal government, Russian regions, and the neighboring former Soviet republic of Georgia had all sent aid that had arrived by yesterday.

Promises, Promises

Excerpts of article by Uri Dan in Jerusalem Post of Thursday, March 25th, 1999

One of the first issues Russian Foreign Minister Igor Ivanov raised after he had welcomed Prime Minister Binyamin Netanyahu and Foreign Minister Ariel Sharon at Moscow Airport was the terror attack last Friday in Vladikavkaz, that killed 61 people and wounded over 100.

In a market similar to that in Jerusalem's Mahaneh Yehuda, Moslem extremists set off some 10 kg. of explosives, massacring innocent people. The attack was apparently committed by a Moslem terror group from nearby Chechnya, a group the Russians say is connected to Osama bin Laden.

Ivanov raised the incident when he told his guests that Russia wants to cooperate in the fight against international terror by Moslem extremists.

The wheel of history takes some ironic turns. From the 1960's to the 1980's, when the Soviet Union was under a totalitarian regime, Israel repeatedly said that in the end, the USSR would itself suffer from the fact that it was training terrorists for the PLO and other groups. But during those gloomy days under Leonid Brezhnev and others in the Kremlin, no one particularly cared to listen.

Today, when the Russians are conducting themselves as a democracy, and as a result have dramatic economic and social problems, the country is suffering from unceasing attacks by Islamic terrorists, who are treading the well-worn and cruel path paved by the PLO, with the Soviet Union's encouragement.

The issue of cooperating in the fight against terror had already been raised with Sharon during his last visit to Moscow in January, when he met with officials from the Russian Defense and Interior ministries, as well as with Ivanov and Prime Minister Yevgeny Primakov.

The Russian security agencies want to link up with Israel on this issue, much as Israel already cooperates with the US and Europe. Friday's attack made the issue even more pertinent.

Perhaps it was this fear of Islamic terror that prompted Primakov to use unequivocal language when Netanyahu and Sharon brought up Israel's objections to the aid Russian firms are providing Iran to develop ballistic missiles and weapons of mass destruction.

"What do you think, we want to commit suicide?" exclaimed Primakov. And he suggested that a committee headed by Ivanov and Sharon work to prevent the transfer of unconventional weapons technology from Russia to Iran.

Of course, Moscow has repeatedly denied American and Israeli claims against it on this issue, and even after it announced it would take action against the firms in question, nothing was done.

But Netanyahu and Sharon, following their talks in Moscow this week, said "This time, it seems as though our Russian hosts have changed their tone and their content.

Primakov and Foreign Minister Ivanov stressed that they really mean to stop this dangerous aid to Iran," our leaders said. "They know it poses a threat not just to the region, but to Russia, itself."

(Victor Mordecai comments: Another very unknown conflict in America is that of the Armenian Christians and their Azeri Muslim neighbors. Also unknown to most Americans is that at the same time the Turkish Albanian's slaughtered 200,000 Christian Serbs in Kosovo in 1915, the Anatolian Turks were slaughtering 1.5 million Christian Armenians in a Holocaust which most of the world is unaware of. Indeed, Adolf Hitler said, "No one said anything about the Turks killing the Armenians in World War I." So, it seems Hitler thought he could get away with killing the Jews in World War II.)

Armenians Mark Victims of Turkish Genocide

Article by Marilyn Henry in Jerusalem Post of Sunday, April 25th, 1999

Yerevan - Armenia - Nearly a half million Armenians yesterday mourned the 1915 massacre by the Turks with a solemn procession through the streets of Yerevan to a hilltop genocide memorial that they lovingly covered with meters of flowers and wreaths.

Early in the cold and overcast morning, groups began to congregate in the capital, organizing themselves by family, factory, school, professional association, army unit and academic institute.

The procession to commemorate the genocide of 1.5 million Armenians began at 10 a.m., when the clock on the main government building chimed the first bars of the Armenian national anthem.

Flags on state buildings flew at half-staff.

The commemoration was expected to end near midnight, when, by official estimates, more than a half million of the country's 3.5 million people would have visited.

"People will walk miles just to lay a single flower," said Rouben Adalian, the director of the Armenian National Institute, a Washington-based organization that documents the genocide.

Only three hours after the first visitor, there was a colorful waist-high hedge of carnations and tulips encircling the eternal flame in the center of the memorial.

Wreaths covered the dozen slabs that ring the memorial, forming a dome open to the sky.

The steady stream to the memorial, on the grounds of the Armenian Genocide Museum, was orderly, dignified and quiet, with virtually no police supervision and without any agency coordinating the massive procession.

On the eve of the commemoration, there was a somber ceremony at the site when soil from the New York grave site of Henry Morgenthau Sr. was interred in a niche in a wall adja-

cent to the memorial. Now, a national hero in Armenia,
Morgenthau, who was appointed as ambassador to the Ottoman Empire by President Woodrow Wilson, is remembered for
protesting - in vain - against the massacre.

Other niches hold soil from the grave sites of a German
Protestant priest, Johannes Lepsius, who documented the Ar-
menian genocide a year later, and Austrian-Jewish novelist
Franz Werfel, who dramatized the event in his novel "The Forty
Days of Musa Dagh."

The ceremony mixed kaddish (Jewish prayer of mourning) and incense. Gersh-Meir Bourstein, a Lubavitch rabbi who
is the chief rabbi of Armenia, and Armenian Orthodox bishops
each said prayers in front of several hundred who gathered in
the rain for the service, including Morgenthau's grandson and
two of his great-grandsons.

The genocide memorial, on a hill with a view of Mount
Ararat, was completed in 1995, on the 80th anniversary of the
massacres.

For many Armenians, the site is a cemetery, as many have
no graves at which to mourn their family members who were
victims of the atrocities in the final days of the Ottoman Empire.

After a 1965 demonstration in Yerevan's Republic Square
by Armenians who, on the 50th anniversary of the genocide,
demanded a memorial, Soviet officials erected a monument. That
site was not inscribed to identify its meaning. It is believed that
Moscow wanted to avoid giving offense to Turkey, which has
never acknowledged the genocide.

Adalian was among the hundreds of thousands of mourn-
ers walking up the hill yesterday. He carried a wreath of white
carnations, in memory of Minas Keusemanougian, his great-
grandfather.

The family name died in Adana (Turkey) in April, 1909,
when Keusemanougian and his sons were among the 30,000
Armenians killed in riots by Turks.

"The genocide was not one single event," said Adalian, a
historian. "It was years of atrocities."

Azerbaijan Reports New Karabakh Clash

Article in the Jerusalem Post of Sunday, June 20th, 1999

Baku (Reuters) - Azerbaijan yesterday reported new clashes on the cease-fire line near its breakaway region of Nagorno-Karabakh, but Karabakh officials deny any fresh fighting.

A statement by the Azeri Defense Ministry said Karabakh rebels had opened fire on Azeri positions with automatic weapons and rocket propelled grenades on Friday evening.

Karabakh, populated predominantly by ethnic Armenians, broke away in 1989 and claims full independence from Azerbaijan.

Azerbaijan blames neighboring Armenian for standing behind the separatists, but Armenia formally denies any direct link to the conflict.

"The Azeri side returned fire on the Armenian positions. There were losses on both sides during the shootings," the statement said.

(Victor Mordecai comments: As part of this Islamic Threat Update, it is needless to say that Iran plays a major role. In my first book "Is Islamic Islam a Global Threat?" I discussed Islamic "hit" teams dispatched around the world, assassinations, internal persecution of Christians and even Iranian Moslem intellectuals and finally the Islamic Republic of Iran's terrorist intelligence and foreign ministry units.

It is hard to believe that prior to 1979, Iran was America's greatest ally in the Middle East and central Asia after Israel. All of a sudden, the country is no longer pro-Western, but has become possessed by the satanic Ayatollah Khomeini. Iran goes through a radical metamorphosis and becomes the greatest enemy of America, Israel and the West. In 1979, during Jimmy Carter's presidency, the US embassy in Tehran is overrun by Islamic students, and the US diplomatic staff taken hostage for over a year. In my first book, I show how these radical students become the leaders of the Iranian Foreign Ministry and worldwide terrorist networks.

The following are a series of newspaper articles updating my first book and re-confirming the pivotal role played by Iran of the Islamic Ayatollahs.)

Former Hostage Anderson Sues Iran for $100 Million

Article by Arlene Levinson in Jerusalem Post of Tuesday March 23rd, 1999

Athens, Ohio (AP) - Almost exactly 14 years since the day he was taken hostage in Lebanon, Terry Anderson and his family filed a $100 million lawsuit against Iran yesterday. The former Associated Press correspondent says Iran sponsored the captors who kept him blindfolded and shackled for more than six years.

Similar lawsuits became possible only in recent years, and at least three have won millions of dollars in judgements. Anderson, now 51 and teaching journalism at Ohio University, also expects to win his case, filed yesterday in US District Court in Washington.

But like the other plaintiffs, he also expects his lawsuit to become a challenge to the US government.

US President Bill Clinton's administration has thwarted claimants from collecting millions of dollars awarded by US courts, even though the damage claims are against countries the US State Department labels as sponsors of terrorism.

In October, the President issued a blanket waiver of a requirement that federal agencies help obtain that money.

"Much of our argument is likely to be with the US government, rather than the Iranian government," Anderson said in an interview at his home about 16 kilometers outside of Athens.

"The law says that the US government is supposed to help us in pressing our claim," said Anderson, who is confident of winning a judgement against Iran. The biggest obstacle to us receiving any money is the White House."

The lawsuit also names as plaintiffs Anderson's wife, Madeleine Bassil, 49, and their daughter, Sulome, who seek redress for emotional distress and their long separation from Anderson.

Sulome, 13, was born three months after her father, then AP chief Middle East correspondent, was taken captive in Beirut on March 16, 1985, as he returned from a morning tennis game.

Held longer than any other American in Lebanon, he was freed 2,454 days later, on December 4th, 1991. The family is seeking $100 million in compensatory damages and unspecified punitive damages.

Named as defendants are the Islamic Republic of Iran and its Ministry of Information and Security.

The lawsuit says Anderson's captors were members of the Hizbullah, and that Iran provided the group "with funding, direction, and training for its terrorist activities in Lebanon.

It says that as a hostage Anderson was fed a poor diet of bread, cheese, and rice; was beaten, taunted, and humiliated; was regularly threatened with death and falsely promised release; heard his fellow captives beaten and one die; grew so depressed he beat his head against a wall until he bled.

Another man held hostage with Anderson in Lebanon, Tom Sutherland, said yesterday he plans to file a similar lawsuit within the next two months. Sutherland, 67, is a professor emeritus of animal science and agriculture at Colorado State University and lives in Colorado. Like Anderson, he was held captive for more than six years.

Iran's UN ambassador, Seyed Mohammad Hadi Nejad Hosseinian, denied Friday that Iran had supported the hostage-takers and said US courts have no jurisdiction over foreign countries.

In a faxed reply to questions, Nejad Hosseinian said through a spokesman that Iran condemns international terrorism and that there is "no shred of credible evidence" that it finances Hizbullah.

Iran as well as Cuba, Iraq, Libya, North Korea, Sudan and Syria are listed by the State Department as state sponsors of terrorism.

Foreign countries used to be largely immune from lawsuits in US courts. The Antiterrorism and Effective Death Penalty Act of 1996 allows legal action against countries alleged to sponsor terrorism that kill or injure US citizens.

Such lawsuits seemed to get a boost last October when Congress required the Treasury and State departments to help recover damages. But an escape clause empowered the president to bar such help "in the interest of national security."

One way of collecting is to go after assets frozen in the US. But the administration is trying to block this avenue.

US National Security Adviser Sandy Berger did not respond to repeated requests for comment on the policy. The State Department had no public comment.

Anderson has little expectation of getting any money either, but explains: "If we don't file a suit, whenever Iran and the United States settle accounts, we won't be sitting at the table."

Iran's Less Pleasant Face

Article by Daniel Leshem in the Jerusalem Post of March 16th, 1999

Italian Foreign Minister Lamberto Dini believes Iran "no longer wishes to be considered an enemy but a responsible regional power." Can Iran indeed be considered a responsible regional power contributing to regional stability?

Gulf Cooperation Council states don't seem to think so. They seem no less concerned about the Iranian threat than about that of Iraq. The UAE, which has repeatedly called on Teheran to accept dialogue or international arbitration to resolve the sovereignty dispute over the three strategic Gulf Islands (Abu Mussa and Greater and lesser Tunb), is in fact more concerned about Iran. The UAE's "Al-Khaleej" daily, which is close to the government, has denounced "the escalation of Iranian provocation" and said that "Iran has closed all doors opened by the UAE to try and find a peaceful solution to the issue of the three occupied islands."

What has most angered the UAE and the GCC has been Iran's recent decision to hold large-scale naval and air maneuvers near the three islands and inaugurate a new town hall on the island of Abu Mussa. These moves were described by the semi-official "Al-Ittihad" daily as "fresh proof of the lack of credibility of Iranian officials' statements that Iran wants to start a dialogue with the region's states... based on mutual respect."

Iran's growing ballistic missile and weapons of mass destruction capabilities, and its accelerated weapons development programs have also raised grave concern among the Gulf states. This has prompted the US to offer them a link to its satellite-based missile launch early warning system, which would supply them with real-time information on either Iranian or Iraqi missile firing tests or attacks.

On his recent trip to Italy, Iranian President Mohammed Khatami was quoted as saying that "Iran has no hostile intentions toward any country or anybody." He added that "the world is weary of terrorism and violence." Yet, he has given his whole-hearted support to his country's long-range ballistic missile development program, which can't be explained just by the Iraqi threat. Baghdad is about 150 km away from the Iranian border (while the Shehab-3 and 4 have ranges of 1,300 km and 2,000 km, not to mention the planned 5,000 km-range missile).

Last August – a few weeks after the Shehab-3 firing test – Khatami defended the development programs, citing especially the Shehab-3 missile, and warning that "Israel constitutes a threat to every country in the region and world, every minute."

This kind of Iranian argumentation didn't make the US less concerned. Last September when the Shehab-3 was displayed in Teheran, President Bill Clinton was probably also informed of the slogans printed on various missile and rocket launchers shown on the parade. They read: "Israel should be wiped out from the map" and "The USA can do nothing."

Similar rhetoric was heard at the recent "Jerusalem Day" rallies throughout Iran, by far, the largest demonstrations in the region.

No less worrying to both Israel and the US are reports that Iran has supplied the Hizbullah in Lebanon with 45 km-range artillery rockets which could threaten the Haifa area.

Iran's Defense Minister Ali Shamkhani recently claimed that Iran has a strategic weapon system intended to "deter Israel." He wasn't referring to the Shehab-3. (Sheikh Fadlallah,

Hizbullah's spiritual leader, has also mentioned a "sophisticated weapon" which, he claims, Iran could use against Israel from Lebanese territory if Israel chose to attack Iran).

Deploying this type of long-range weapon in Lebanon is the best proof of Iranian irresponsibility and massive support of terrorism. If this isn't proof enough for the Europeans, then all they need to do is to read the report of Argentine Judge Juan Jose Galeano, chief investigator into the bombings of the Israeli Embassy and the Jewish community center in Buenos Aires, who found Iran responsible for these demonic attacks.

(Victor Mordecai comments: On April 18th and April 19th, 1998, two newspapers, "Yediot Ahronot" Israeli Hebrew language daily and "The New York Times," respectively, published first page headlines about a 22 ton shipment of Russian scud missile parts stopped on their way to Iran at the Azerbaijan border with Iran. The difference between the two articles was that the Israeli paper described the scud missile parts as being highly radioactive. Since the steel missile casings are not radioactive in their natural state, they had to have been irradiated by a nuclear warhead or some other radioactive source. Did the warhead get through? How many other missiles may have gotten through? I highly recommend to my readers that they acquire a video of the movie "The Peacemaker." This shows just how easy it is to smuggle missile and nuclear technology from the former Soviet Union into Iran. In my first book I described Iranian nuclear capabilities. Could this be the "sophisticated weapon" the Irans gave the Hizbullah in Lebanon mentioned above?)

Argentina: Islamic Jihad Bombed Embassy

Article from the Jerusalem Post of Wednesday, May 12, 1999

Buenos Aires (AP) - Argentina's high court said Monday the pro-Iranian Islamic Jihad was responsible for the 1992 Israeli Embassy bombing that claimed 29 lives here, according to local media reports.

A statement by the Supreme Court of Justice did not elaborate on what evidence it had implicated Islamic Jihad, the local news agency "Diarios Y Noticias" reported.

The court also said its evidence pointed to an explosion originating outside the building, and not within the embassy as some earlier reports suggested. No suspects have been detained in the investigation. Israel has long contended that Iranian groups were behind both the 1992 attack and a 1994 bombing of a Jewish cultural center here that killed 95 people. Teheran has repeatedly denied involvement.

In Jerusalem, the Foreign Ministry released a statement expressing satisfaction at the development. "Seven years after the terrorist attack on the Israeli Embassy in Buenos Aires, the Supreme Court of Argentina has ruled that the explosion occurred outside the embassy grounds and that the Islamic Jihad, an arm of Hizbullah, is connected to it. Israel views the ruling as a positive development which will now enable the investigation to continue, focusing on the search for those responsible and on possible accomplices within Argentina."

Iranian Students Protest Murders of 5 Writers

Article on page 7 of the Jerusalem Post of Wednesday, December 16th, 1998

Teheran (AP) - More than 1,000 university students, protesting a wave of mysterious murders of dissidents, yesterday called for the dismissal of Iran's chief judge and the heads of the intelligence and security services.

Earlier, some 3,000 writers, poets and artists attended the funeral of one of the five dissidents, Mohammed Mokhtari, whose body was found on the outskirts of Teheran last week. He had apparently been strangled.

Two dissidents remain missing. Students at the rally at Teheran's Amir Kabir University blamed the hard-line officials for indirectly encouraging violent incidents by not condemning or trying to stop them.

Iran's Khatami Ousts Security Chief

Article by Jonathan Lyons in the Jerusalem Post of Wednesday, February 10th, 1999

Teheran (Reuters) - Moderate President Mohammed Khatami took a major step yesterday to extend his authority over Iran's powerful secret police, after a string of dissident murders threw his conservative rivals on the defensive.

Teheran state television reported Khatami had officially accepted the resignation of Intelligence Minister Zorbanali Dorri Najafabadi from the post of minister for intelligence," the television said in its main afternoon news bulletin, confirming preliminary reports in several Iranian dailies.

It did not name a successor, but press reports say it will be Ali Yunesi, chief of military tribunals and head of a special commission formed by Khatami to investigate several mysterious murders of nationalist politicians and secular intellectuals.

Yunesi, like the outgoing minister, is a Shi'ite cleric.

Under Iran's Islamic system many key powers, including the final say in military, security and foreign policy, lie with the country's supreme clerical leader and not the elected president.

By placing his own candidate at the head of the intelligence services, Khatami could significantly strengthen his position.

The television said the president had thanked Dorri Najafabado for his service to the nation and asked him to remain in his post until a replacement could be named and sent to parliament for ratification.

Khatami's allies had demanded Dorri Najafabadi's removal since startling public admissions early last month, prompted by the president's investigation, that rogue elements inside the intelligence ministry had helped carry out the grisly murders.

The killings sparked widespread public revulsion in Iran, with many pro-reform newspapers pointing the finger at hardliners out to undermine Khatami's bid to create a civil society at the expense of traditional clerical power.

In his resignation letter, the minister said he was leaving his post "to create the suitable atmosphere and necessary conditions for this powerful ministry to carry out its duties."

But it was clear Dorri Najafabadi felt he had been hounded from office in the wake of the murders, which the presidential commission ruled were the work of rogue agents and not linked to any of Iran's mainstream factions or senior officials.

"The recent painful events... led to ruthless attacks by domestic and foreign enemies against the country's great security and intelligence apparatus and its hard-working and dedicated personnel," he said.

Khatami, a moderate cleric, had been given little room to maneuver by rival conservatives when he filled the sensitive intelligence post while forming his cabinet in August 1997.

Iranian media said at the time that Dorri Najafabadi had been the president's 15th choice.

But the hardliners, who earlier cautioned against a rush to judgement or other hasty action that might undermine national security, had recently begun to abandon the intelligence chief.

On Monday, newspapers quoted a leader of parliament as saying the largely conservative body would not obstruct any attempt by Khatami to replace the minister, a clear signal that a deal was in the works.

"If Mr. Khatami wants to remove the intelligence minister, the parliament will put forward no opposition," said influential conservative Mohammed Reza Bahoner. Under Iranian law, all cabinet members must be confirmed by parliament.

Iranian Dissident Death Suspect Kills Self

Article in the Jerusalem Post of Monday, June 21st, 1999

Teheran (Reuters) - A central suspect in a series of murders of Iranian intellectuals and dissidents has committed suicide in jail, complicating a top secret case involving intelligence officers, a senior judicial official said yesterday. The suspect, identified as Saeed Emami, killed himself on Saturday by drinking a "hair-removing" solution while taking a bath in prison,

Mohammed Niazi, the head of the country's military tribunals, told the official IRNA news agency.

Iran Suicide Victim Was Top Agent - Reports

Article by Mehrdad Balali in the Jerusalem Post of Tuesday, June 22nd, 1999

Teheran (Reuters) - A key suspect in a series of murders of Iranian dissidents and intellectuals, who committed suicide in prison over the weekend, was a top intelligence agent, newspapers said yesterday.

Saeed Emami, was accused of masterminding the killings late last year of four opposition leaders and dissident writers, in which rogue elements of the intelligence ministry where implicated.

Judicial officials said he killed himself on Saturday by drinking a hair-removing solution while taking a bath in prison. "Salam" daily said Emami, known in security circles as Saeed Eslami, had served for years as a deputy intelligence minister.

Emami, who was a student in the United States, had returned to Iran two years after the 1979 Islamic revolution to work for the country's intelligence apparatus, newspapers said. He moved up the ranks of the ministry under former intelligence minister Ali Fallahiyan who is sought by German authorities for his alleged role in the 1992 murders of Kurdish dissidents in Berlin.

The moderate daily "Salam" said Emami had been opposed to the 1997 election of reformist President Mohammad Khatami. The investigation ordered by Iran's top leaders including Khatami, led to the resignation of intelligence minister Qorbanali Dorri Najafabadi in February.

Emami was among a number of secret agents arrested and many others questioned in connection with the sensational top secret case, which has become all the more complicated with the reported suicide.

Revelations that secret agents had a part in the killings shocked the nation and led to a bitter factional dispute.

Reformers backing Khatami linked the murders to right-wing squads supported by his conservative political rivals, while hard-liners blamed some of the president's allies at the Intelligence Ministry, as well as foreign espionage networks.

"The prison authorities should have exercised closer watch on a person like this. Emami could have propelled the case forward with greater speed, but now many of the things he knew will remain unsaid," said Mohammad Atrianfar, a reformist member of Teheran City Council who is a top Khatami ally.

Others suggested a possible cover-up and questioned the ease of committing suicide in Iranian jails, where they said prisoners are tightly guarded.

The Iranian Mirage

Editorial of the Jerusalem Post on Thursday, June 24th, 1999

Once upon a time, when there was a nation called the Soviet Union, there was a branch of political science informally called "Kremlinology." This peculiar pursuit involved making judgements about the inner workings of an enigmatic dictatorship based on guesswork over who was up and who was down, who was a "moderate' and who was a "hard-liner." The Soviet Union is gone, but "Kremlinology" lives on in other contexts, such as Western attempts to peg foreign policies on the vicissitudes of internal Iranian politics. Accordingly, we are told that President Mohammad Khatemi is a "moderate" who must be encouraged in his struggle with the dark forces of the "hard-liners," who still dominate the government.

The problem with this mode of thinking is that it can easily help perpetuate the dictatorship that the West thinks it is cleverly undermining. It has taken the arrest of 13 Jews on charges of espionage to remind the West that, "moderates" notwithstanding, it is too soon to pronounce the Iranian regime reformed.

The arrests of the Jews took place in March, but since their disclosure by Iranian officials this month, an impressive international campaign has been launched for their release. Even

Arab nations such as Saudi Arabia and Jordan, have been approached by Western governments and Jewish organizations. So far, neither quiet diplomacy nor public pressure has worked.

According to a delegation of Israelis originally from Iran who met Monday with Ashkenazi Chief Rabbi Yisrael Lau, Iran has arrested more Jews, bringing the total to 22. Information is sparse regarding the prisoners, since Iranian officials only permit them visits from children aged five to seven.

Lest there be any doubt regarding the precariousness of the Jews' situation, it should be noted that 17 Iranian Jews have been executed since the Islamic revolution of 1979. If convicted of espionage, the Jews currently in prison will be executed.

The dilemma of the West in confronting this situation is essentially that of the police advising the family of a kidnap victim. Rather than pay ransom in the form of economic inducements, however, the West should restore the policy of isolation that was being quietly discarded. The $200 million in recently thawed World Bank projects that had been frozen since 1993 should be refrozen. The US should return Iran to the top of its terrorist-sponsors list, especially since CIA Director George Tenet recently testified that Iran's support for terrorism has not lessened.

Congressional sanctions on Iran should be enforced, not waived.

In short, the Clinton Administrations famous "dual containment" policy - of which little remains of either its Iranian or Iraqi pillars - should be resurrected. The policy of making Teheran's life easier in the hope that Iran will respond by moderating its behavior has been tried, and has failed. The alternative is to continue expressing desire for cooperation, but implement all sanctions strictly until Iran changes its behavior.

The argument that a tougher approach toward Iran will "play into the hands of the hard-liners" is both familiar and flawed. First, there is little evidence to back the idea that the West can understand, let alone micromanage, the internal politics of a closed regime. Second, even if there is a division between moderates and hard-liners, the way to help the moderates is to increase the price attached to hard-line policies.

Veterans of the human rights struggles with the former Soviet Union, such as Natan Sharansky, remember well a similar debate over the Jackson-Vanik amendment. In that bitter debate, advocates of detente fought against imposing economic sanctions to open the gates for Soviet Jewry. A similar argument raged between backers of "constructive engagement" with South Africa's former apartheid regime, and proponents of stiff economic sanctions.

Though in retrospect few would argue with the critical role played by economic sanctions in the Soviet and South African cases, the lessons of experience have yet to be fully applied to Iran. The lesson is that the more the West indulges the commercially driven efforts to alleviate the financial woes of rogue regimes, the longer those regimes will be able to postpone their collapse.

The only way to help the imprisoned Iranian Jews is to ensure that the cost to Iran of their execution is extremely high. The only way to help the Iranian people and safeguard Western security interests is to link sanctions to actual behavior, not to misguided attempts to cultivate mirages of moderation.

World Bank Halts Iran Loans Due to Arrests

Article by Jeremy Pelofsky in the Jerusalem Post of Thursday, June 24th, 1999

Washington (Bloomberg) - The arrest of 13 Jews in Iran for alleged espionage has prompted the World Bank to halt preparations to loan $200 million for sewers and health care projects in Iran, the "Washington Post" reported, citing unidentified World Bank officials.

World Bank lawyers were planning to go to Teheran soon to discuss the loans with the government - drawn up initially in 1993 but put on hold - until those plans were postponed indefinitely after the arrests, the newspaper said.

The loans won't likely be considered this year, an unidentified official told the Post.

The World Bank has previously approved about $720 million in loans for Iran, of which about $307 million hasn't been disbursed, according to the bank's 1998 annual report.

(Victor Mordecai: To end this section on a "lighter" note, I have chosen the following article from the Jerusalem Post of Sunday April 11th, 1999.)

Iran Cartoonist May Face Court for Drawing

Teheran (Reuters) - An Islamic revolutionary court ordered the daily "Zan" closed last week after it published a contentious cartoon.

The court summoned editor Faezeh Hashemi, daughter of former president Rafsanjani, and told her to bring the young cartoonist with her, the newspaper "Neshat" said.

Hashemi insisted 17 year-old Davood Ahmadi Mounes had merely drawn what he had been told to. It shows a thief holding a couple at gunpoint while the husband advises the gunman to shoot his wife because he would have to pay less blood money.

Under Islamic law, relatives of a murdered woman receive only half the amount of blood money paid for a male victim.

Algeria Says 100,000 Dead in Seven Years' Strife

Article on page 5 of Jerusalem Post of Monday, June 28th, 1999

Algiers (Reuters) - One hundred thousand people have died in Algeria's seven-year conflict between Moslem guerrillas and the government, state-run radio said yesterday.

The conflict has also left an additional one million victims, the radio added in an apparent reference to people who have been wounded or lost homes and relatives. It quoted President Abdelaziz Bouteflika as giving the figures during a visit to Switzerland where he addressed an economic forum in Crans Montana yesterday. The figures were the first comprehensive toll that an Algerian government has given since the conflict began in early 1992 when authorities cancelled a general election in which radical Islamists had taken a commanding lead.

(Victor Mordecai comments: On page 170 of my first book "Is Fanatic Islam a Global Threat?" I quoted an article in the New York Times International Edition by Bob Herbert of September 30, 1997 that the total number of dead in Algeria had reached an estimated 60,000. Again, it must be emphasized that there are no Jews or Christians in Algeria on whom this killing can be blamed. This is a classic example of what will happen in any Islamic "Dar es-Salaam" or "utopia" where everyone is Moslem. The Islamic system is a "black hole" or self-destructive system as we can see from countries like Algeria, Afghanistan and Sudan.)

The Invisible War

In remote terrain, two million Sudanese have died. Others are being enslaved. The fighting has lasted for decades, and no one is trying to end it.

Excerpts of article by William Finnegan in "The New Yorker" monthly of January 25th, 1999, pp. 50-73

Since Sudan gained its independence, in 1956, "the Arabs" - that is, a long series of Muslim-led governments, civilian and military, elected and otherwise - have been fighting a civil war against non-Muslim black rebels in the South. (The only significant break in the fighting lasted from 1972 to 1983.) At present, the government controls little territory in the southern third of the country - mainly just a string of garrison towns - and the rebels of the Sudanese People's Liberation Army largely hold sway there.

There are said to be six hundred ethnic groups in Sudan, speaking some four hundred languages and its suits the government to have a maximum number of armed bands roaming around, raiding their neighbors and generally preventing the South from forming a united front against the North.

Obscure, and chaotic, and low-tech as it is, the civil war in Sudan is a disaster of historic proportions. Altogether, it has killed more than two million people, according to the latest figures - by some estimates, more than any other conflict since the Second World War. The great majority of the dead have been civilians in the South. Partly because southern Sudan is one of the world's poorest, least accessible regions, news coverage of the war has been light.

Sudan is not the only country in Africa whose borders seem to have been perversely drawn, sealing enough ethnic and historical enmity within them to insure a future of civil war. It is however, the largest country in Africa, covering more than a million square miles. The fact that it stretches from the Nubian and Libyan deserts, where it shares borders with Egypt and Libya, to the rain forests of central Africa, where it borders on Congo and Uganda, has helped condemn its people to unusually harsh and intractable strife since independence.

Before this century, the main basis of the relationship between the Muslim North and the non-Muslim South of today's Sudan was, moreover, a busy slave trade: some two million southerners are thought to have been taken north as slaves during the nineteenth century alone. This profoundly bitter connection might even be described as the underlying reason that the two regions find themselves in the same modern nation.

In the latter half of the nineteenth century, the Ottoman Empire, responding to British pressure and employing British administrators, tried to stamp out the slave trade in the Sudan, provoking, in 1881, a rebellion among the local Muslims, who also objected to the corruption of Ottoman rule. These rebels were the Mahdists, who took Khartoum, beheaded General Charles Gordon in 1885. Mahdist rule, at its peak, apparently extended up the White Nile as far south as the present-day border with Uganda, and included all of Dinka country. After the British re-conquered the region, in 1898, the colonial boundaries hardened largely where centuries of slavers had established them.

The British administration, to be sure, treated northern and southern Sudan as if they were separate countries. Infrastructure development was directed almost exclusively to the

North, while the South was administered under a closed-door policy that included expulsion of Arab traders and discouragement of the spread of Islam. Christian missionaries were allowed to work in the South, and graduates of the mission schools tended to go farther south, to Kenya and Uganda - rather than to Khartoum - for college. The future of southern Sudan was seen, both by the British and by the emerging mission-educated southern elite, to lie with black East Africa rather than with the Arab North. Things did not turn out that way, mainly because of the great determination of northern nationalists to take the South with them when they charted their course for independence. The northern leadership failed almost entirely to consult with the southern leadership about the terms of independence, and the first round of civil war started four months before the Union Jack was even lowered.

That round of warfare lasted seventeen years and took half a million lives. It finally ended, in 1972, with an agreement that gave the South a large degree of self-government and control over its natural resources, which were soon discovered to include oil. In 1983, Khartoum tore up the agreement. General Ja'afar Nimeiri, an erratic leader who had come to power in a 1969 military coup, stripped the southern legislature of its powers and decreed that the southern oil would be refined in a northern city. What was more, Nimeiri, who had become a fanatic Muslim, ordered that Islamic shariah law be applied throughout the country. This meant that even non-Muslims would be subjected to the often ghastly punishments of hudud (which include amputation of limbs and stoning to death) for such crimes as adultery and drinking alcohol. By then, southern soldiers had mutinied, and the SPLA was launched.

Nearly two million southerns have died in the current round of the civil war, either directly from the fighting or from war-related famine and disease. Four million others have been driven from their homes - some into neighboring countries, many into the North. Although there are no reliable figures - Sudan's population is estimated to be around thirty million, but the country's last accurate census took place in 1956 - the South's population has probably declined since 1983, when it was believed to be around five million.

Many observers have used the word "genocide" to describe Khartoum's conduct of the war. The government's destruction of villages, targeting of civilians, and obstruction of international relief supplies to desperate sometimes starving populations in the South have been widely documented. Perhaps the strongest case for a charge of genocide, however, exists in the Nuba Mountains, which until recently were the only theater of the war not in the South. The Nuba people are a congeries of black African tribes who inhabit a fertile range of hills in central Sudan, surrounded by plains-dwelling Arabs. The SPLA opened a front in the area in 1986, and government's response has been notably brutal: of an estimated total of a million Nuba, more than half have been displaced, and more than a hundred thousand are believed to have perished.

Living conditions in the South, always difficult, have deteriorated drastically. Very few people now have access to clean water, and diseases - cholera, malaria, hepatitis, measles, kala-azar, leprosy, sleeping sickness - kill many thousands each year. Few schools, few hospitals, and few roads remain open. Land mines are ubiquitous. Famine, a constant threat in subsistence economies during wartime, strikes quickly when crops fail or must be abandoned or when people's cattle or goats are stolen. In 1988, a devastating famine following a drought killed a quarter of a million people and in 1989 an international relief consortium called Operation Lifeline Sudan was established to deal with the country's seemingly permanent humanitarian emergency. OLS, which today consists of two UN agencies (UNICEF and the World Food Program) and forty non-governmental organizations, operates on both sides of the civil war, having access agreements with the SPLA and the Sudanese government.

Neither side in the conflict seems able to strike a decisive blow. The leadership of the Sudanese government has changed hands twice since the SPLA's war against it began - Nimeriri was deposed in 1985, and the civilian government that followed was in turn overthrown by a 1989 military coup backed by radical Islamists. Colonel (later Lieutenant General) Omar Hassan Ahmad al-Bashir led the 1989 coup and became President, but the maximum leader of the revolutionary regime he installed was a and remains a former law-school dean named Hassan al-Turabi.

The Turabi regime banned most "non-religious institutions," such as labor unions and political parties, and ruthlessly repressed dissent. Some former Sudanese officials - the Islamists purged nearly eighty thousand members of the Army, the police and the state bureaucracy - joined the rebels. A number of neighboring countries, among them Uganda, Eritrea, and post-Mengistu Ethiopia, noting that Sudan had begun aiding armed opposition groups from their countries, began to lend support to the SPLA. Some not so neighboring countries, such as Israel and the US, noting that Sudan had become an important haven for international terrorists, including the now famous Osama bin Laden, also grew better disposed toward the rebels. In late 1997, Madeleine Albright even met with John Garang, the SPLA commander, in Uganda.

The US, having added Sudan, in 1993, to the list of countries that it believes sponsor international terrorism, imposed comprehensive economic sanctions in 1997. Nevertheless, the Turabi regime has managed a vast arms buildup, obtaining weapons from, among other countries, China, Russia, Iran and Iraq. This buildup has come on top of a large preexisting base of military hardware provided, ironically, by the US during the Cold War, when Sudan was seen as an anti-Soviet bulwark against Ethiopia.

Although local cease-fires are called to allow for famine relief, and the government has rewarded defecting SPLA senior commanders with comfortable jobs, even Cabinet-level posts, few serious negotiations to end the war have taken place in the nine years since the Turabi regime seized power. The Islamists' determination to win the civil war militarily - the leadership constantly refers to the conflict in the absolutist terms of jihad - has devastated not only the South but also the northern Sudanese economy.

The government, while trying to run one of the world's poorest countries, spends more than a million dollars a day on the war. Its Army now has seventy-five thousand regular troops, eighty-five thousand reserves, and fifteen thousand active irregulars. These irregulars - and they do not include many tribal

militias armed by the government, or thousands of troops still
under former SPLA commanders, who retain their independence
- fight, for the most part, in Iranian-trained militias called
People's Defense Forces, which are among the most feared units
in the war. The PDF militias specialize in bloody raids against
southern civilians, and in some areas they have helped reintro-
duce that old staple of North-South relations in Sudan: slavery.

It was mid-afternoon, and while I was hiding from the heat
in my tukul (hut) a young man came to fetch me. An Arab had
brought more than a hundred villagers back from captivity in
the North, he said - local people who had been taken as slaves
in May.

The Arab said he came from El Da'ein, a Rizeigat town
some two hundred miles north of Nyamlell, in Darfur Province.
He said his name was Ibrahim Muhammad Hamdan - although
when I asked if that was his real name he admitted it wasn't.
What he was doing, he said, was extremely dangerous. The government had been coming to El Da'ein to recruit for the PDF.
'They take normal people and train them to come and loot in
the South," he said. "They arm them and tell them, 'Kill the
young men, but bring back the cattle and the women.' I even
have PDF looters in my own family. But many people in El Da'ein
don't agree with the government. They don't want the war. They
say, 'If the South must secede for us to have peace, then let
them secede.' But you cannot say that publicly, or you will be
killed."

It seemed that in previous years the Arab and his team
had transported escaped slaves back to Twic County, in Dinka
country, about a hundred miles east of Nyamlell, and that they
had been paid for their trouble by a group called Christian Solidarity Worldwide. The president of Christian Solidarity Worldwide is Baroness Caroline Cox, of Queensbury. Did I, by any
chance, know Lady Cox? Her organization had paid fifty US
dollars for each returned slave.

Gathering that I did not know - and did not know even
how to contact - Lady Cox, the Arab grimaced with disappoint-
ment. In the end, he said in a resigned tone, he and his team
might have to accept whatever the families of the escaped slaves
could pay.

Khartoum must be one of the world's least charming old capital cities. Its shabbiness is monumental, its amenities remarkably few, considering that it is home to some five million people. The main streets are filled with choking dust and diesel fumes. The old villas are disintegrating, and the newer buildings are blindingly ugly. Parks are rare and unkempt. Even the banks of the great rivers - the Blue Nile and the White Nile meet in Khartoum - remain, for the most part, muddy and dispiriting. In architecture and public planning, Islamist theory seems to make little provision for the modern commons. The result, in Khartoum, is a city of walls, as residents retreat from the harsh neglect of the streets into private realms - into whatever they can afford in the way of gardens, patios, a shuttered house.

Khartoum is also a city of rumors. Hamas, I heard, was on the fifth floor of my hotel - the Hilton. But I only ever saw members of a Libyan soccer team, lithe in bright-blue sweatpants, get off the elevator at five. German businessmen, looking hot and unhappy, sat in the lobby waiting for government officials. Gulf State sheikhs swept past, too important to wait for anyone, and disappeared into white limousines. Above all, in the Hilton and around Khartoum and everywhere in government-controlled Sudan, there was the mukhabarat, the secret police, watching, listening, bundling the truly unfortunate off to their jails and torture centers, terrifying everybody.

It was stupefying, somehow, after being in the South, to know that Khartoum, this Middle Eastern desert city, parched and puritanical, was the putative capital for the myriad tropical African societies of Equatoria and Dinka country. But even the apparent homogeneity of the "Arab" and "Muslim" North is an illusion. There are no pure Arabs in Sudan - each tribe of Arab nomads who ventured south of Egypt over the past couple of millennia mixed with local people, and the Arabic-speaking riverain Sudanese who today describe themselves as Arabs are usually quite dark-skinned. They are the country's largest ethnic group, but they are not a majority - amounting to only forty per cent of the total population, according to the 1956 census. (Dinkas, at twelve per cent, are the second-largest group.) Although Islam is the state religion, only sixty per cent of Sudanese are Muslims, and though Arabic is the country's official language, only sixty per cent of the people speak it.

The Rise of a radical Islamist movement in Sudan was strictly an elite phenomenon, building slowly among university students and the professional and political class in Khartoum before and after independence, and in direct opposition to an equally small, well-educated Communist movement. The Islamists in Sudan gather much of their political and financial strength from an international group known as the Muslim Brotherhood, which promotes political Islam throughout North Africa and the Middle East. In 1986, during the last election before their 1989 putsch, Sudan's Islamists, known then as the National Islamic Front, received eighteen per cent of the vote. (It was their highest vote total ever but still well behind the votes of both the big Sufi parties. These parties, both basically family dynasties, are currently underground, with their exiled leaders in armed alliance with the SPLA.) They have functioned in power as a vanguard part, and it seems safe to say that if a free election were held today they would get even fewer votes.

And so the prospects of the full-scale mobilization for war that was under way while I was in Khartoum in October seemed to me dubious. The universities had effectively been closed. There was strong resistance to the general call-up, especially among university students, but almost nothing appeared in the press about it. And there was great apprehension among parents of young men liable for conscription: everybody I talked to mentioned it, and stories about hospitals in Juba and Khartoum filling up with the newly wounded were circulating furiously. Few people seemed to be buying the idea, much repeated by the war's promoters, that dying for jihad in the South was a glorious way to go, and that all such martyrs received a swift transfer to paradise.

But there also seemed to be little feeling among ordinary people in Khartoum about the war itself - that is, little real support for the war, and little serious criticism of it. People seemed ready to discuss, and even passionately denounce, the government - assuming that the mukhabarat was not around - but the war was of much less interest. The South was a primitive, impoverished waste, according to most of the people who could be bothered to discuss it with me. Unless I was mistaken, a great many northern Sudanese would be just as happy to let the whole place go.

People felt keenly the loss of political freedom under the Islamists. The previous government might have been corrupt and ineffectual, but at least it had been elected. This regime banned political parties, labor unions, and public meetings. It shut newspapers and magazines, and it harassed its opponents without mercy. Thousands had disappeared, and millions had fled the country. The mukhabarat had expanded enormously, and a national network of "popular committees" had been created by the region to act, among other things, as spies on ordinary citizens.

The regime's roughest side is, of course, the mukhabarat, which is really a myriad of agencies, many with their own detention centers (even the state electricity agency has its own detention center), staffed mainly by semiliterate thugs and torturers. Torture centers are known in Sudan as "ghost houses."

The Turabi regime's smoothest side is Dr. Turabi. He has been a prominent Islamist since his university days, in the early nineteen-fifties. He held advanced law degrees from the Sorbonne and the University of London and in the early sixties he was the dean of Khartoum University's law school. He was jailed for seven years during the Nimeiri dictatorship, then released and later made Attorney General. He was a prime mover in Nimeiri's imposition of shariah law, and he was still a close Presidential adviser in early 1985, when Nimeiri disgusted much of the Muslim world by executing Mahmoud Muhammad Taha, a distinguished liberal scholar of Islam, who was then in his seventies. Indeed, Turabi's path to power is said to be littered with a large number of bodies. But knowing much about this Machiavellian, not to say bloodstained, curriculum vitae only leaves a visitor to Turabi's office unprepared for the lissome, laughing old intellectual who presides there.

"We are going for freedom, completely," he told me. He waved his hands in a loose, fluttering circle and giggled. Dark-skinned, white-bearded, and wearing white robes, a turban, and black-framed sunglasses, Sudan's maximum leader is - with his little buck-toothed, Bugs Bunny laugh - an improbable figure.

He is also given to making improbable arguments. At one point, he was trying to convince me not just that his poor, hungry, war-torn backwater "is becoming a very important country" but that his terrifying police state "is a free country," and added, "Monopoly is only for God." He mixes economic libertarianism with high-flown disquisitions on art, science, and religion. ("An artist is submitting to God. A scientist is doing the same.")

The overall impression is of a politician so hardheaded, so shrewd in his assessments of enemies and allies, and ultimately so successful in his machinations that he can afford to be playful, obscure, even silly. I found his single most unnerving gesture to be an upward-glancing, inward swoon of contemplation followed by a girlish sigh.

I asked Turabi about the war. He said that John Garang was jealous of the former rebels who had joined the government, which struck me as unlikely. To explain the situation in the South to me, Turabi thought to use an American analogy - the Civil War. "The Confederacy no longer exists," he said. "Most of the niggers of yesteryear, they are in Chicago now. It is just the same here, with millions of southerners having come to the North. With better roads, which we plan to build, virtually all of them will come North. They are becoming conscious of the fact that there is such a thing as a job, etc. They will no longer want to sit under a tree just waiting for the fruit to fall."

The idea that the people of Sudan's South - herders and farmers with the most physically demanding lives imaginable, people as deeply wedded to their lands as any set of tribes on earth - are lazy and are looking forward to moving north en masse to work for the hated Djellabah struck me as so deeply foolish that it was almost funny. Nobody laughed, though. And Turabi nattered on.

Not only is Sudan's civil war, as presently arrayed, unwinnable by either side but peace itself seems to lack any significant constituency. Suffering, war-weary civilians have little leverage. None of Sudan's neighbors are being seriously threatened by the war. In fact, few, if any, of their governments, no matter how much they fear and loathe Khartoum, and no matter what they say publicly in support of the SPLA, want to

see the South win its independence. All of them have their own
restive minorities, and secession is thus a horrifying idea.

Egypt, the regional powerhouse, detests the Turabi regime.
(Egypt's government does, anyway. The country's many Islamists tend to feel differently.) In August, Cairo hosted a meeting
of the leadership council of John Garang's National Democratic
Alliance, and in September President Mubarak announced,
against most available evidence, that the American attack on
the Al Shifa pharmaceuticals plant in Khartoum had been justified. And yet even the Egyptian government has no interest in
seeing southern Sudan gain its independence.

Egypt's overriding strategic concern is the Nile, without
whose waters it cannot survive. The last thing Cairo wants to
see is a weak new southern state, possibly under the influence
of Israel, controlling most of the upper White Nile. This is never
publicly stated, but it is widely understood. Indeed, it is often
given as the reason that Garang doesn't dare announce that the
SPLA's real goal is independence for the South: Egyptian opposition would doom his movement. Of course, the viability of an
independent southern state is another question. Landlocked,
with virtually no infrastructure, and already filthy with war-
lords, it would be the world's poorest country - completely destitute, even by African standards, and totally dependent on outside investment for any development. If there is any sunnier,
more realistic prospect for an independent South, I haven't heard
about it.

American policy toward Sudan since the end of the Cold
War - and since the rise of the Turabi regime - has been a combination of open hostility, stemming mainly from the regime's
involvement with Iraq and from its hospitality toward a remark-
able number of terrorist groups; of humanitarian engagement,
primarily through Operation Lifeline Sudan; and of tepid political support for the rebel alliance. Like Sudan's neighbors,
who aid the SPLA and would seemingly like to see the regime
in Khartoum fall, Washington does not appear to have any actual alternative government in mind. The fact is that Sudan's
strategic significance to the US today is negligible, with the Horn
of Africa no longer a cockpit of American-Soviet competition.
Egypt is our key regional ally; Sudan is a sideshow.

Given the scale of Sudan's suffering, the ongoing catastrophe of its civil war, and the millions of lives already lost in the South, the geopolitics raise an extremely disturbing possibility. While the outside world's obliviousness of Sudan's plight is real, it is hardly complete. There is, after all, Operation Lifeline Sudan, now the largest air-relief operation since the Berlin airlift, fifty years ago. OLS is expensive, having so far cost its sponsors more than two billion dollars. For the price of one week's air relief, it is sometimes said, all the war-destroyed bridges and roads in the South could be repaired. Such reconstruction would, of course, require peace. The hard question is why the international community - the Western powers, really, led by the US - is willing to invest so heavily in humanitarian relief and, at the same time, to invest almost nothing in the diplomatic effort that might compel the warring parties to make peace. The awful possibility is that the Sudanese status quo, an indecisive, low-intensity conflict that weakens an unfriendly regime and suits our key regional ally, Cairo, also suits our policymakers.

And so I heard our Martin Mawiens Dut, the village magistrate in northern Bahr al-Ghazal who had recently lost his wife, his daughter, and his son in the war, as he explained his hopes for an American-sponsored, all-parties peace conference for Sudan. "Only the Americans can do it," he had proclaimed. "We are all counting on them!" And I did not tell him what I had heard one analyst say - that West, for market reasons, would probably become interested in Sudan's oil reserves in about thirty years, and that Sudan should therefore expect its civil war to last until then.

An Uneasy Calm in Egypt

Article by Ben Lynfield in the Jerusalem Post of Friday, April 16th, 1999.

In the Cairo neighborhood of Imbaba, Sheikh Gaber and his followers are a bad memory.

For several years in the late 1980's and early 1990's, Gaber's backers, some of them armed, held sway over part of

Imbaba, enforcing Islamic observance and imposing their own version of law and order.

In 1992, Egyptian security forces mounted a campaign to retake the area, with casualties incurred on both sides. Hundreds of militants were arrested, including Gaber.

Since then, the government has kept calm in the area by keeping many of the militants behind bars and maintaining patrols by security forces, according to residents. It has also provided - for the first time - a small share of services, including asphalting the streets.

"Some [militants] are here but there aren't any problems with them" says Issam Ahmed, 27, a storekeeper. "Many of them are in prison, and some of those experience a healing of their minds."

The campaign in Imbaba came early on in what has turned out to be a fierce seven-year battle between the Egyptian state and Islamist proponents of violent change.

In recent years, the militants appear to have been increasingly set back by the security forces, though they proved their continued striking capability with the November 1997 massacre of 58 tourists and four Egyptians at Luxor.

The struggle has claimed more than 1,200 lives - security forces, militants and civilians according to the "Al-Ahram" weekly newspaper.

Throughout the country, including Upper Egypt - the main flashpoint of the conflict - there has been a pronounced drop in the level of violence in recent years, says Saad Eddin Ibrahim, head of the Ibn Khaldun Center, a Cairo think-tank. Sometimes, months go by without any incidents, he says.

Moreover, leaders of the largest militant organization, Al-Gama'a al-Islamiya, have, since July 1997, issued several calls on members to desist from anti-government attacks in apparent acknowledgment of the high costs of the armed struggle.

The most recent statement, issued on March 25th, followed earlier appeals to the rank and file for a cease-fire from six Gama'a leaders imprisoned in Egypt and Sheikh Omar Abdel-Rahman, the group's spiritual leader, who is serving a life term in the US for plotting to blow up the World Trade Center.

"I think they are in retreat in many domains," Hala Mustafa, an analyst at the Al-Ahram Center for Political and Strategic Studies, says of the militants.

But they remain a threat, she says. To sustain a victory, she believes, the government will have to undertake political reforms and foster further economic development.

The outcome of the battle against the militants promises to shape the future of President Hosni Mubarak's regime, because it touches on all policy areas - economic, political and diplomatic.

The government is currently implementing an economic privatization and stabilization program in which attracting foreign investment is a major goal. A prerequisite for that is stability.

Tourism, the country's greatest foreign-currency earner, is only now bouncing back from the damage inflicted by the Luxor massacre.

In domestic politics, the battle against the Islamists has offered a rationale for retaining emergency laws and curbing civil liberties. In foreign policy, the militants challenge the government's adherence to the peace treaty with Israel and its close relations with the US.

The government has gotten the upper hand almost exclusively by military means, and has also benefited from splits among militant leaders and public disillusionment with them, Mustafa and Ibrahim say.

The leaderships of Gama'a and Gihad, the other leading violent group, have split in to three factions: those in prison, those abroad, and those inside Egypt who are still at large, says Ibrahim.

Moreover, says Mustafa, the image of the militants has taken a beating in recent years, partly because of their egregious acts of violence.

"They are not seen as saints or an idealistic power, as they used to present themselves," she says.

The Islamists also face an ideological crisis because the Iranian regime, which served as their model, is now riven by splits and internal conflicts, she adds.

There is also, of course, the military explanation for the militants' woes: Security forces have increasingly gained intelligence and experience that enabled them to improve their performance in the battle, says Ibrahim.

And especially after the Luxor massacre, Cairo was highly successful in gaining extradition of wanted militants from countries within and beyond the region.

Amnesty International has, over the years, repeatedly criticized the Egyptian government for its methods in combating Gama'a and Gihad, including trials of civilians in military courts, detentions of suspects for years without trials, use of the death penalty, and alleged systematic use of torture.

Egypt has denied violating human rights.

The two militant groups have extremely bloody track records: assassinations of ministers and intellectuals, a 1995 attempt by Gihad to kill Mubarak, repeated killings of Coptic Christians, and massacres of tourists.

During one attack in 1996, Gama'a gunmen killed 18 Greek tourists. The group later issued a statement that they had mistaken them for Israelis.

The idea that Islam is the solution for society's ills and that the government should rule according to Islamic law has deep roots in Egypt.

The Moslem Brotherhood, the inspiration for Islamist movements throughout the region, was founded in Ismailiya in 1928.

Its history has been one of violent confrontations with the state, interspersed with periods in which there were degrees of accommodation. The brotherhood has been outlawed since 1954, when members tried to assassinate president Gamal Abdel-Nasser.

Towards the end of his rule, Anwar Sadat facilitated the growth of the brotherhood and other Islamist groups as a means of counterbalancing a perceived challenge from leftists. He was assassinated on October 6th , 1981, by Moslem militants serving in the army.

During the first decade of the Mubarak regime, the brotherhood, in addition to cultivating its vast network of voluntary and charitable organizations, was able to gain control of professional syndicates and student unions and to gain entry into parliament in alliance with the Liberal and Labor parties.

After the wave of attacks began in the early 1990's, the government increasingly viewed the brotherhood as a political foil to Gama'a's use of violence.

A key question now is whether Gama'a's ceasefire announcements are tactical or strategic, a respite or a break from the past.

Diaa Rashwan, also of the Al-Ahram Center, argued in a recent Al-Ahram article that a "pacifist" trend is on the ascendant in Gama'a and that the group may soon issue a new charter supplanting its advocacy of violence.

But Mustafa does not discern any radical changes in the militant organizations.

"Sometimes they depend on their military wing and sometimes on political organizations. They have both sides. For the time being, they don't have any option other than a cease-fire because they want time to rebuild themselves and to gather students and supporters again."

To achieve a real victory, the government needs to target underlying causes of militancy such as unemployment, income inequities, and lack of political participation, says Ibrahim.

It remains to be seen, he adds, whether the 5 per cent economic growth rate that Egypt is currently experiencing will translate into more jobs for the poorest sectors of the population.

The government, for its part, is raising such expectations.

"Mubarak to visit industrial area in Assiyiut," trumpeted front-page headlines in government affiliated papers last month, referring to a conflict-torn area in Upper Egypt. Eighty-five projects in the works there will provide "16,000 jobs for young graduates," the papers said.

"New projects are giving people hope," says Ibrahim. "But if the hopes don't materialize there could be a backlash and a flare-up again."

In Ibrahim's view, a move towards fair elections that would give a genuine mandate to those elected is essential.

Elections for Egypt's People's Assembly are notorious for being rigged, and voter turnout is extremely low. In the last balloting, held in 1995, Mubarak's National Democratic Party won 95% of the vote.

It is "probably" time to allow the Moslem Brotherhood a political voice, Ibrahim believes.

"It has turned into a peaceful organization over the last 25 years," he argues.

Until now, the Brotherhood's aspirants have run as independents or in alliance with other parties.

But Mustafa views legalization of a Moslem party as a blueprint for trouble.

"We forget that we need first to secularize," she says. "You can't talk about full democracy without a degree of secularization in the society."

In her view, boosting secularization and developing a tolerant political culture will require education, media efforts and giving liberal forces a greater chance to express themselves.

Alluding to the victory of the Islamic Salvation Front in Algeria's 1991 elections and the subsequent civil war, Mustafa says: "I don't think the model of Algeria is the best model to copy."

Cracks in the Pyramids

A book review by Shimshon Arad of "A Portrait of Egypt" by Mary Mary Anne Weaver in the Jerusalem Post of Friday, April 2nd, 1999

Even when their prognosis is basically valid, prophets of doom are seldom persuasive. Mary Anne Weaver's new book falls into this category. She first arrived in Egypt over 20 years ago to enroll at the American University of Cairo as a graduate student in Arab affairs. Confessing no Middle Eastern ancestry nor any preconceptions, she was determined "to get through to the Egyptians and to try to see them as they see themselves."

Thus began her personal journey through the world of militant Islam. It was, she found out, "a strange, always human, sometimes violent, unpredictable road." Her objective was "to trap the spirit of Egypt." The canvas she paints is that of a very troubled country on the verge of cracking. But is she right in her judgment? Students of Egypt are not quite sure whether she has fully grasped the resilience of the Egyptian riddle.

Her story starts in 1977, as Sadat flew on his first visit to Jerusalem. Weaver witnessed the student union elections that were held at Alexandria University, elections that would prove to be a turning point. Islamist associations swept the boards, taking control of the prestigious faculties of medicine, engineering, pharmacy, and law, where they immediately began to impose their will, forcibly preventing the teaching of Darwin and forbidding the celebration of the secular national holidays.

What puzzled Weaver at the time was why so many of her fellow students, "wealthy, sophisticated, chic Cairenes," spent their summers in military training in desert camps. It turned out that they were part of the swelling camp of militant Islam.

Weaver soon discovered that the Islamists had also begun to infiltrate university faculties and had set up clandestine campus cells. They were demanding the abrogation of all Western influence in the schools and had begun publishing a large number of newspapers and tracts. Their funding came largely from Saudi Arabia, and with Sadat's consent. But why? Sadat, and later Mubarak, thought that encouraging the Islamists would contain the leftists. She alludes to how, in the late '70s and early '80s, Israel supported Hamas in Gaza, thinking erroneously that it would block the rise of the PLO.

Islam's militant revivalist movement was born in Egypt 70 years ago, when Hassan al-Banna founded the Moslem Brotherhood. He recognized no separation between church and state, rejected secularism and called for the abolition of Egypt's Napoleonic legal code. Among the many drawn to the Brotherhood in its early years were Nasser and Sadat.

However, after Nasser seized power in 1952, the honeymoon between his regime and the Brotherhood was short-lived. The Brotherhood continued to agitate for an Islamic state, and its members also conspired to assassinate the new ruler. In 1954, the Brotherhood's leaders were executed or tortured and the organization was banned. Over 4,000 of its members ended up in concentration camps.

Following Sadat's assumption of power in 1970, Communists and Nasserites were interned and many Islamists were released. Saudi Arabia donated $100 million to help the Islamic campaign "against Communism and atheism." Apart from the Moslem Brotherhood, other organizations began to dominate the Islamic trend. The first was known as Gama'a al-Islamiya, with the blind Sheikh Omar Abdel-Rahman as its spiritual leader. The second was al-Jihad, whose military wing later perpetrated the killing of Sadat. Today's militant Islamic movement consists of more than 40 organizations, all of which came of age on university campuses during the '70s.

Sadat's assassins were part of an underground army cell of al-Jihad, led by a former colonel in military intelligence, but also including Lieutenant Khaled al-Istambouli, the actual killer, Sheikh Omar Abdel-Rahman, and an electrical engineer who was it s chief ideologue. Weaver maintains that an alliance of Egypt's military, civilian and religious life constitutes an ominous reality. Sadat's killers justified their action under Shari'a law. For reasons not quite clarified, Sheikh Omar was set free.

During a visit to Egypt in 1993, Weaver found that Sheikh Omar's power base had continued to expand, while his underground army had begun to engage in increasingly violent acts against Mubarak's regime. Mubarak's "repression was a response to the militants' accelerated assaults" on Copts, intellectuals, the police and foreign tourists.

Looking always for the cause of this eruption of Islamic militancy, Weaver found plenty of them. Firstly, the huge influx of American funds since the peace treaty with Israel. There was easy money, a more ostentatious lifestyle for a small number and the growing misery of the majority. She found an angry country, crumbling cities, and crowded mosques. Entire neighborhoods in Cairo would suddenly turn silent: it was time for worship. Many women were wearing abayias, and cassettes of sermons by Sheikh Omar were everywhere.

Secular Cairenes were worried about the growing polarization of political life, and there was mounting concern about the Islamist movement. She heard almost universal criticism of the government's response. Weaver also encountered "a tangible fear that Egypt could lose its struggle against militant Islam." The Moslem Brotherhood was possessed of both substantial power and great wealth; the growth of Islamic banks had been phenomenal, controlling sums estimated at between $2 billion and $3 billion. There was also a proliferation of Islamic social-welfare institutions, including day-care centers, hospitals and schools, and increasing Islamic influence in the media, the arts, and the courts.

The most anguishing question was (and still is): To what extent have the Islamists infiltrated the armed forces and the security services? Ambassador Hussein Amin, a career diplomat and a "prominent intellectual, who has taken a publicly critical view of the militants," believes that an Egyptian Islamic state is inevitable. Unfortunately, "economic and social reforms can never catch up with the rising Islamic tide."

This thesis has been repeated by many others. Weaver asked Mustafa Mashour (who in 1996 became the leader of the Moslem Brotherhood), what the Brotherhood's strength was in the Army. He hesitated and did not reply directly, but then said: "The Army is religious, it's part of the people and it's close to Islam as we are." Banning the Brotherhood played into the hands of the more extreme militants.

When Weaver managed to get an interview with Sheikh Omar in a New York jail, he admitted that the Islamists want "a true Islamic state," close to the example of Sudan. A Western ambassador told Weaver that, "unlike Algeria, Egypt's Islamist groups are not regime-threatening - at least, not yet." Mubarak, claimed that ambassador, "keeps insisting that they are a creation of Iran and Sudan." Weaver does not buy that assertion, and she is probably right. Despite Mubarak's pronouncements, said the anonymous ambassador, "the problem is not Iran or Sudan. It's him."

Weaver asked Mubarak what concerned him the most about the problems facing Egypt. "Our main concern is the economy," he said. As for the Islamic "fanatics," he said: "They are nothing to worry about. We are used to this in Egypt. It goes up and down. This problem of terrorism throughout the Middle East is a by-product of our own illegal Moslem Brotherhood - whether it's al-Jihad, Hizbullah in Lebanon, or Hamas." Mubarak went on to assert that the violence in Egypt began when the veterans of the Afghanistan war returned home.

And yet, as "ruthless as Mubarak is" in dealing with militant Islam, he continues to condone Islamist influence in those places where perhaps it has the greatest impact. Government's brutal crackdown on militant Islamic foes has cleared most of the country of acts of terrorism, but Egypt's Islamist militancy, though outmaneuvered and repressed, has a way of reappearing. Which has led Youssef Chahine, who is Egypt's most accomplished filmmaker, to assert that "the atmosphere is pretty electrified; it's becoming pretty vicious down there."

(Victor Mordecai comments: In "Is Fanatic Islam a Global Threat?" I stressed that there is a domino theory at work here. Iran was the first country to fall to fanatic Islam in 1979. Then came Afghanistan and Sudan in the 1980's. Saudi Arabia, though not a fanatic Islamic state officially has been spending billions of dollars to spread Islam as we can see from the above articles. In my opinion, Islam is not moderating but growing, spreading and becoming more radical both in Islamic countries as well as the West. Ambassador Hussein Amin comments that an Egyptian Islamic state is inevitable. This reinforces my fears that Egypt indeed will be just another domino to fall to Islam. What does that say about the peace process with Israel? Especially after Israel has returned the Sinai to Egypt three times for peace? Will Egypt then attack Israel again a fourth time across the Sinai?)

Congressmen Seek Mubarak's Help in Ganani Case

Article on page 2 in the Jerusalem Post of Sunday, March 28th, 1999.

Six US congressmen have signed a letter to Egyptian President Hosni Mubarak saying their support for US-Egyptian trade may be conditional on the restoration of money owed to Dvora Ganani-Elad, an Israeli businesswoman expelled from Egypt in 1997.

Ganani-Elad, the first Jewish Israeli businesswoman in Egypt, was expelled from Egypt shortly after the Azzam Azzam spy affair, four years after opening a profitable import-export business. Previously, she had served as a consul for tourism in the southeastern US.

According to the legislators' letter, she was "forbidden to return to her home and offices in Cairo. She was unable to bring her financial affairs to a proper close. And her lawyers in Egypt disposed of her property and liquidated her financial assets. They then kept Ms. Ganani-Elad's funds for themselves."

The congressmen urged Mubarak to rectify the injustice and concluded that such cases "Make our support for Egyptian-American trade difficult to endorse when we meet with businesses in our congressional districts and in Washington."

The signatories included Lincoln Diaz-Balart, Carrie Meek, Ileana Ros-Lehtinen, Robert Wexler, E. Clay Shaw, and Benjamin Gilman.

The following four newspaper articles deal with European and global aspects of the Islamic threat.

In The Netherlands, Neglected Churches Are Given New Use

Excerpts from article by Marlise Simons on page A8 in the New York Times International Section of Monday, March 18th, 1997.

Amsterdam — Every Friday afternoon, a courtyard along a busy Amsterdam street fills with Muslim men parking their bicycles and removing their shoes as they prepare for prayers. They may not see it this way, but the worshipers at the Fatih Camil Mosque are part of a fundamental change in the Netherlands.

The site where Allah is now loudly praised used to be a Roman Catholic church. It has been stripped of its crosses and paintings, and the spires on its two plump towers now carry a crescent moon.

But it is not Islam brought here mainly by Moroccan and Turkish immigrants, that is troubling the Dutch priests and pastors. Rather it is a more far-reaching shift, the continuing decline of Christianity.

Dwindling church attendance by Catholics and mainstream Protestants has forced the clergy in much of Europe to confront the same, often painful question their counterparts in New York and other American cities have asked: What to do with the cavernous churches, the myriad chapels and sprawling monasteries that have become redundant and require small fortunes to keep up.

Disused churches can be found in Britain, France, Germany, and many are simply closed. German churches, though, are supported by tax revenues, and French churches long ago became municipal property, all of which help pay for maintenance.

But in the crowded Netherlands, where the churches own the buildings and space is precious, the response has been pragmatic and secular.

Cash-strapped church elders have sold off more than 250 places of worship in the last two decades, buildings were Catholics, Calvinists and Lutherans had prayed for a century or longer. Many have already been converted into libraries, shops, cultural centers and even apartments and discotheques.

Some changeovers signal another kind of transition. A handful of churches were bought by young evangelical sects, New Age groups, and growing Muslim communities.

Jews have followed the trend, though on a smaller scale. One community sold a little-used 18th century synagogue in the Hague, and it was recently dedicated as a mosque. Another synagogue in Amsterdam, houses the Resistance Museum. A third is being turned into a store.

The Dutch Government's national heritage foundation often pays part of the conversion costs, particularly if it involves one of the 2,300 places of worship listed as protected. Protected or not, the churches are seen as part of the neighborhood, as a vital part of the urban landscape, said Gaap het Hart, director of the foundation.

"They do not want them demolished or changed," he said. "But as the country goes on secularizing, there is less and less money available to keep the buildings going."

In much of Western Europe, church attendance has been slipping since the 1960's, dropping particularly fast in the 1980's. Among the Dutch, the decline has been especially steep. While in 1960, 18 per cent of the Dutch said they belonged to no church or religion, in 1995 that number had reached 40 per cent, according to the national Bureau of Statistics.

The steepest drop has been among Protestants, who are split into various denominations. Catholics remain the single largest group, making up 33 per cent.

The dismantling of the churches has produced anxiety and soul-searching among parishioners, even in a country that tends to be more practical than emotional. Religion may seem irrelevant to many people, but the power of its images and symbolism endures.

Selling property has sometimes put religious elders in an awkward position. When a Muslim group wanted to buy the big 18th century synagogue on the Wagen street in The Hague to use it as a mosque, the Jewish community opted for a go-between: It first sold the building to the city, which then sold it to the Muslims.

Of the country's nearly 40 Orthodox synagogues, only about a dozen are in use. Almost three of four Jews who lived in the Netherlands before World War II died in the Holocaust. Today many do not practice the faith.

More than 125 Catholic churches have been closed since 1973, but just as many smaller ones have been opened that allow for more versatile use as community centers. The old buildings have been much in demand as mosques, because of their large size. But the archdiocese hesitates to sell them to Islamic groups, after a few "difficult" experiences, Mr. Klok said.

"Islam has many currents, and you end up dealing not with a religious group but with the government behind them," he said.

In Utrecht, for instance, the Emmaus Church was being transferred ostensibly to an Islamic foundation. "It turned out we were dealing with the Libyan Government," Mr. Klok said.

Swiss Back Refugee Limits
Measure is Approved Amid Influx From Kosovo

Excerpts from article by Elizabeth Olson in the International Herald Tribune of Monday, June 14th, 1999.

Geneva — Fearful of too many refugees flooding into the country, Swiss voters on Sunday overwhelmingly approved tighter rules for asylum seekers.

Voting as part of Switzerland's direct democracy system, citizens cast more than 70 percent of ballots in favor of the government measures designed to deal with increasing numbers of refugees, particularly from Kosovo. The measures limit reviews of individual refugee cases.

Already home to about 180,000 ethnic Albanians from Kosovo, Switzerland has been experiencing an enormous influx of refugees fleeing the turbulent province. With arrivals up by 60 per cent over last year at this time, Switzerland is expecting as many as 60,000 refugees by the year's end, giving it the highest number per inhabitant in Europe.

"The government measures allow collective admission for certain groups of refugees, such as ethnic Albanians from Kosovo. However, this wholesale shelter limits refugees' right to make their case for individual persecution, which is necessary to be granted permanent asylum in Switzerland.

In addition, refugees without identity papers can be ejected more quickly under the new controls.

"There is a side to Switzerland that is very generous, giving millions to refugees," said Christian Levrat of the Swiss Organization for Aid to Refugees in Bern, "and a stricter side that wants to make sure that people coming in are not abusing the law."

Voter approval was strongest in the German-speaking part of Switzerland, where Kosovo Albanians have been denounced in newspapers as criminals and drug dealers, although the measures sailed through in the French-speaking portion of the country as well.

Radical British Moslem Activist Arrested

Article from the Jerusalem Post of March 16th, 1999.

London (Reuters) — Fundamentalist Moslem activist Abu Hamza Masri was arrested yesterday under Britain's Prevention of Terrorism Act, a spokesman for Masri'a London-based Supporters of Sharia organization said.

A police spokeswoman confirmed that three men were being held after a series of raids by anti-terrorist detectives. The suspects were taken to a central London police station. Police have so far not named the men.

A group representing British Moslems, the Muslim Parliament of Great Britain, urged that Masri be given "due process of law" during his arrest.

Despite what it called Masri's "exaggerated and irresponsible" statements in the last few months, the Moslem body said no evidence had so far been produced to substantiate his involvement in acts of violence or terrorism.

Egyptian-born Masri, who has a distinctive metal claw replacing one of his hands, has been vocal in encouraging Moslems worldwide to fight for a more Islamic way of life. He is reported to have close links with Middle East activists.

His son and stepson were arrested late last year in Yemen in connection with hostage-taking and bomb-plot charges.

From his base at the North London Central Mosque, where he is the imam, Masri runs his Islamic activist organization and a web site which has a link to Saudi-born dissident Osama bin Laden's 17 page fatwa, or death threat, against the United States and other "enemies of Islam."

Bin Laden Said Planning New Attack

Top Alleged Terrorist Charged
in US Embassy Bombings

Article by John Diamond in the Jerusalem Post of Friday, June 18th, 1999.

Washington (AP) — A week after the FBI put him on its 10 Most Wanted List, suspected terrorist Osama bin Laden is said by US intelligence to be in the advanced stages of planning another attack.

Though the timing and location of the strike are unknown, a US official said there have been indications in recent weeks that bin Laden has been moving unspecified materials that could be used in a terrorist operation, and that US facilities in African nations such as Ghana or Mozambique could be targets.

Blamed by the US for ordering last year's bombings of US embassies in Kenya and Tanzania, bin Laden is thought to be in Afghanistan, where the FBI said is getting no help in bringing him to justice.

Bin Laden has openly declared his hostility to the US for its support of Israel and for the presence of US troops in the Gulf region.

Because of the difficulty of launching an operation at targets in the US, bin Laden is expected to focus on targets in poorer countries where security is weaker, intelligence officials have concluded.

But the official stressed that there is no clear intelligence on the timing or target of any impending attack. The official, asking not to be identified, said terrorist threats have been received on all continents.

Meanwhile, Ayman Zawahiri, the reputed leader of the terrorists who killed Egyptian president Anwar Sadat, was charged Wednesday in a conspiracy to kill Americans that included efforts to secure "the nuclear bomb of Islam."

He was charged with conspiracy in the bombings of embassies in Kenya and Tanzania, as was Khaled Fawwaz.

The indictments raises to 15 the number of people charged in the August 7th, 1998, bombings that killed 213.

The indictment, which supercedes a previous indictment, claims that three days before the embassy bombings, Zawahiri threatened to retaliate against America for its capture of members of his group, Al-Jihad. It also alleges that bin Laden, accused of orchestrating the embassy bombings, issued a May 1998, statement titled, "The Nuclear Bomb of Islam." The statement said that "it is the duty of the Moslems to prepare as much force as possible to terrorize the enemies of Allah," according to the indictment.

Zawahiri, believed to be with bin Laden in Afghanistan, allegedly leads Al-Jihad, an outlawed group that had claimed responsibility for the 1981 assassination of Sadat. It has been waging a bloody campaign since 1992 to topple President Hosni Mubarak's government and install strict Islamic rule. Fawwaz is in custody in London awaiting extradition. Bin Laden was last known to be hiding in Afghanistan.

The following two articles deal with Palestinian and Islamic threats to Israel's security.

Major Smuggling Tunnel Exposed in Gaza

Article by Arieh O'Sullivan on page 4 in the Jerusalem Post of Thursday, June 10th, 1999

The Israel Defense Forces displayed a major tunnel discovered between the Gaza Strip and the Egyptian border town of Rafah, suspected of being used to smuggle merchandise, drugs, fugitives, and possibly weapons.

It was the sixth and most sophisticated tunnel discovered so far this year, having lighting, a telephone system, air conditioning, and a small rail line running from end to end, like in a coal mine.

The army said the 75-meter long tunnel extended beneath the Israeli-controlled border fence and road which splits the town of Rafah.

"You can't walk upright in it, since it's only 90 centimeters high, but the tunnel had carts which moved smoothly along the rails," said one military source.

The tunnel was discovered some eight meters below the surface by an Engineering Corps "tunnel hunting" crew operating along the border. The IDF uses sophisticated sonar devices in its intensive efforts to locate tunnels, but military sources said this one was found by digging a shaft. Journalists were taken to the gaping pit which broke into the tunnel, but not to its entrance. The IDF has discovered 23 tunnels in the area during the past two and a half years. It usually blows them up, but has not yet decided how it will deal with this one. IDF officers have criticized the Palestinian Authority for not helping to put an end to the tunnel digging.

The Hamas Planned to Poison Israel Drinking Water Sources

Excerpts from article by Michal Goldberg on page 2 of Israel's Hebrew Daily "Yediot Ahronot" of June 18th, 1999 — translated by Victor Mordecai.

This information was revealed from an interrogation of Mohammed Abu Tir, one of the Hamas's military wing leaders in Jerusalem, who was arrested shortly after the deaths of the Awadallah brothers. They also planned to poison swimming pools.

The Hamas planned a mass killing of Israelis by poisoning drinking water sources as well as swimming pools by means of chemicals. Behind these plans was Adel Awadallah, commander of the military wing of the Hamas who was killed together with his brother, Imad, in September 1998.

This was revealed from the interrogation of Muhammad Abu Tir (48) one of the heads of the military wing of the Hamas in Jerusalem, who was arrested shortly after the killing of the Awadallah brothers in a confrontation with an IDF force in the Mt. Hebron region. His trial will begin shortly.

From the interrogation, it was revealed that Awadallah planned a series of mass murders. He purchased weapons such as a mini-Uzi, AK-47 Kalatchnikov semi-automatic rifle and three pistols supplied to him by the owner of a building supplies store in Bethlehem.

"Adel explained that he and others had reached a high enough level to produce chemical materials capable of causing massive deaths. Drinking water sources and swimming pools would be targeted.

Abu Tir also told investigators that a large shipment of weaponries, originating from Iran arrived in Israel via the Dead Sea. The shipment included RPG rockets, bombs, Kalatchnikov and M-16 rifles with telescopic sights.

Chapter Seven

Eschatology

With the rise to power in Israel of Prime Minister Ehud Barak, many people ask how will this new leader of Israel affect the future, the future of the peace process, and the future of the world.

In my first book, I dealt with the fanatic Islamic threat to the world. I showed how Islam had armed itself to the teeth with over a trillion dollars of weapons of mass destruction over the last twenty-six years since the Yom Kippur (October) War of 1973. I showed how a peace process has developed with Israel making peace agreements with Egypt, Jordan, and the Palestinians. Israel has returned not 93% of the lands it was forced to take in two wars of self-defense in 1967 and 1973, as I mentioned at the Dallas Council of World Affairs in 1991, but 97% with lands being surrendered to Jordan and the Palestinian Authority for the sake of peace.

Yet the Clinton Administration and the globalists laugh in the face of UN Resolutions 242 and 338 calling for compromise from both sides and the creation of "secure, recognized and defensible" boundaries. Even more incredulous is the demand of the Palestinian side as well of President Clinton to resettle millions of Palestinian Diaspora Arabs in what is the "core" Israel of today, which would lead to the destruction of Israel plain and simple. The Palestinians have stopped talking about UN Resolutions 242 and 338 and have begun speaking again about the dead and buried UN Resolution 181 of 1947 calling for the partition of Palestine into Jewish and Arab states. The Arab states and the Palestinians rejected this then and waged war with the fledgling Jewish states, and they lost.

The following three articles deal with European demands for a Palestinian state within one year, Jerusalem as the capital of the Palestinian state, Resolution 181, and former Foreign Minister Ariel Sharon's rebuttle of this.

Arabs Pleased By EU Police on Palestinian Authority State

Article on page 2 of the "Jerusalem Post" of Sunday, March 28th, 1999.

Damascus, Syria (AP) —Arab nations yesterday praised the EU's call for Palestinian statehood within a year, with an official Syrian newspaper describing it as "an important step."

"No doubt this declaration of the European Union... and its stress on the Palestinian right to self-determination and establishing a state, form an important step at this time," the state-run Al-Thawra newspaper said.

In Jordan, Foreign Minister Abdul Ilah Khatib described the EU statement as a "positive development and very important for achieving a just and lasting settlement to the peace process."

"The move in the end will receive unanimous global support," he added in remarks carried by the official Petra news agency.

The European leaders' strongest support yet for Palestinian statehood came Friday at the end of their three-day summit in Germany. In a statement, they said that Israel should fulfill the "unqualified Palestinian right" to independence within a year.

Doing so, the leaders said, "would be the best guarantee of Israeli security."

The "Khaleej Times" of the United Arab Emirates said the European Union's backing of Palestinian statehood was significant for its wording and timing.

"The declaration is the strongest affirmation so far by the European community of its belief in the inalienable and unrestricted right of the Palestinians to self-determination," the independent newspaper said.

Egyptian newspapers quoted Foreign Minister Amr Moussa as saying that Egypt welcomed "Europe's confirmation that the Palestinian people's right to self-determination cannot be vetoed by any party, and that final status negotiations should be held without jeopardizing that right."

Moussa, quoted by the semi-official "Al Ahram" newspaper, stressed "the right of the Palestinian people to establish a state with Jerusalem as its capital on all its national soil."

He said that was "an indisputable matter for Egypt and the Arabs, and peace could not be comprehensive or just without realizing that goal, and without an Israeli withdrawal from the Golan Heights and south Lebanon."

PLO: Israel Must Explain Annexation of 1948

Article by Marilyn Henry on page 2 of the "Jerusalem Post" of March 28th, 1999.

New York — The PLO observer to the UN last week appeared to increase the Palestinians' territorial claims when he challenged Israel's pre-1967 borders and called Israel's rejections of the frontiers outlined in the 1947 UN partition plan "pathetic statements involving illegal positions."

"We believe that Israel must still explain to the international community the measures it took illegally to extend its law and regulations to the territory it occupied in the war of 1948, beyond the territory allocated to the Jewish State in Resolution 181," PLO Observer Nasser Kidwa said in a letter, dated Thursday, to Secretary General Kofi Annan.

"Such a situation has not been accepted by the international community," Kidwa said. He acknowledged that although the partition plan was rejected at the time, they later accepted it as part of peacemaking with Israel.

The PLO is saying for the first time that "even the cease-fire lines of 1949 are not acceptable," Israeli UN Ambassador Dore Gold said Friday.

The Palestinians are attempting to use Resolution 181, the UN partition plan, "to make territorial gains inside what has unquestionably been sovereign Israel, as well as to broaden Palestinian claims in Jerusalem," Gold said.

The contratemps at the UN has been brewing in the last week since Gold, citing prime minister David Ben-Gurion, called the partition resolution "null and void."

The Foreign Ministry also has objected to a provision in Resolution 181 that says Jerusalem should be a "corpus separatum," or separate entity, under a special international regime.

Sharon Launches Campaign to Counter EU Jerusalem Letter

Article by Danna Harman on page 1 of the "Jerusalem Post" of March 14th, 1999.

Foreign Minister Ariel Sharon has ordered diplomatic missions to launch an information campaign on the subject of the nations sovereignty over a united Jerusalem. The move came in response to the European Union's restatement of its non-acceptance of Israeli rule over all Jerusalem.

In addition, Prime Minister Benjamin Netanyahu said he plans to suggest a resolution by the cabinet today rejecting the division of Jerusalem under any circumstances, accompanied by a letter to be sent to the EU explaining that its reliance on UN General Assembly Resolution 181 (the partition resolution of 1947, which deems Jerusalem a separate entity from the Jewish state it recommends be created in Palestine) is unacceptable.

Ambassador to the UN Dore Gold explained that "Resolution 181 was made moribund by the violent rejections of the Arab League and not by the decision of the State of Israel."

Gold added that Resolution 181 like all UN resolutions, "Is a recommendation only and does not constitute international law."

Meanwhile, Sharon sent a message to German Foreign Minister Joschka Fischer over the weekend, saying that "notwithstanding the bonds of deep friendship that exist between our two countries, we cannot but reject the content of the note verbally sent by your ambassador on behalf of the European Union... concerning the status of Jerusalem."

In the note, received at the Foreign Ministry last week, German Ambassador Theodor Wallau wrote that as far as the EU is concerned, Jerusalem is not considered to be under Israel's sovereignty, and therefore Israel's call for foreign diplomats to stop meeting with Palestinian officials in east Jerusalem would not be met.

"Dear Colleague, may I reiterate to you in the most sincere yet firm manner Israel's determination — a determination shared by all shades of opinion in Israel — not to allow Jerusalem to become, once again, a divided and separated city," wrote Sharon. "Just as all of Israel shared in your rejoicing at the reunification of Berlin, so we hope and trust that Germany... will accept Israel's reunified capital in Jerusalem."

As can be seen from the above articles, Israel is being forced by world Islam and the globalists to return all 100% of the territories including Jerusalem, or else(!). After that is accomplished, they want to force Israel into the even smaller partition map of 1947.

Even with the election victory of Prime Minister Ehud Barak on May 17th, 1999, I don't believe that any Israeli government will be able to acquiesce to what the Islamic-globalist side really wants, because it will all lead to the piece by piece destruction of Israel, as we have scene precedents these last few years with the systematic destruction of the Christians and Christian interests of Yugoslavia, Sudan, Indonesia, China, and other areas.

I believe the pressures on Ehud Barak will be terrible during the remaining months of 1999. One of the subjects not covered in my first book is the Y2K problem. It is one of the reasons I have written this, my second book. It is part of the strategic equation which I fear (and pray I'm wrong) will spark a new round of fighting before January 1st, 2000.

The following three articles from the "Jerusalem Post" give a taste of some of the Y2K related security threats facing Israel and the world.

Article by Jim Abrams in the "Jerusalem Post" of Thursday, February 25th 1999

Washington (AP) — The Year 2000 computer problem could cause serious disruptions abroad, including breakdowns in nuclear reactors and strategic missile systems, midwinter power outages, and disruptions in world trade and oil shipments, a CIA official warned yesterday.

Air Force Gen. John Gordon, deputy director of the CIA, emphasized at a Senate Armed Services Committee hearing that gaps in information make it hard to assess the scope of the damage in foreign countries, although it is evident that most countries, particularly Russia, are far behind the US in preparing for the crisis.

Gordon said Russia has exhibited a low level of awareness for the "Y2K" problems that could occur if computers misread the year 2000 as 1900. Midwinter power outages, he said, could have "major humanitarian consequences" in countries such as Russia and Ukraine.

"We currently do not see a danger of unauthorized or inadvertent launch of ballistic missiles from any country due to Y2K problems," he stressed. But he said there could be serious local problems with missiles if temperature or humidity monitors malfunction, and that problems in early-warning systems could lead to incorrect information.

The developing world faces the greatest threats of disruptions, Gordon said. China will probably experience failures in key sectors such as telecommunications, electric power, and banking.

The US is regarded as the world leader in fixing the Y2K problem, but the draft of a report being prepared by two senators who have been studying the issue, Robert Bennett, R-Utah, and Christopher Dodd, D-Conn., said the consequences within the country should not be underestimated.

Y2K Bug May Cause Dimona Evacuation

From page 4 of the "Jerusalem Post" of Thursday, May 27th, 1999

The Israeli government is preparing to evacuate all 30,000 residents of the city of Dimona in case of "millenium bug" failures in the computers at the Dimona nuclear reactor, according to the London-based newsletter "Foreign Report." Concern is focused on September 9th — 9.9.99 — which is regarded as the crucial date for testing whether the reactor's computers are 2000-compliant. According to a source quoted by the newsletter, computer experts reported successfully solving 95 per cent of the millennium bug problems. But the government demanded a plan that is 100 per cent foolproof and insisted on a contingency plan if a fail-safe solution could not be found. The Prime Minister's Office had no comment.

Computer Terror Can't Be Ignored

Article by Yonah Alexander on page 8 of the "Jerusalem Post" of June 14, 1999.

The latest "Melissa" virus, which spreads via infected e-mail, and the upsurge of computer intrusion by hackers into the Web sites of the White House, Senate, and the FBI, have once again focused attention on cyber-crime and its ominous international security implications.

It should be recalled that in February 1998, Ehud Tenenbaum, an Israeli hacker also known as the "Analyzer" worked with two young collaborators from California to mount cyber-attacks against the Pentagon's systems, a nuclear weapons research lab and other significant targets.

The prevailing assessment of intelligence agencies, strategic thinkers, and scientists is that not only hackers and "crackers" (criminal hackers) but also terrorists — individuals, groups, and state sponsors — are likely to exploit the vulnerability of the world's computer systems to conduct electronic warfare.

It is estimated, for instance, that hostile perpetrators, with a budget of around $10 million and a team of some 30 computer experts strategically placed around the globe, could bring the US to its knees.

The threat of electronic terrorist assaults grows with each passing day. There are three reasons for this:

* The globalization of the Internet. Internet users currently number over 120 million: an estimated 1 billion people will be using it by the year 2025. This makes efforts to control Internet attacks a daunting challenge to intelligence services and law-enforcement agencies.

* There are now some 30,000 hacker-oriented sites on the Internet, making the tools of disruption and destruction available to almost anyone. The easily available recipes for these new weapons — worms, Trojan horses, and logic bombs, among others — are making this form of warfare a permanent fixture of international life.

* With the Cold War now behind us, terrorist organizations have cast off the limitations and ideologies of the formerly bipolar world and have become multidirectional. These new political realities, coupled with easily accessible cyber-weapons, have enhanced the threats posed by terror groups to the degree that they could alter life on our planet forever.

The Internet already serves as an arena for propaganda and psychological warfare. Ideological extremists such as neo-Nazi groups have called for ethnic, racial and religious violence. Traditional terrorist organizations, like Hizbullah, which is supported by Iran and Syria, maintains on its Web site a daily record of "heroic" battles of its fighters in southern Lebanon. And Afghanistan, the newest state sponsor of terrorism, pushes its radical brand of Islam on-line.

Terrorists have also used their laptops to store operation plans. Ramzi Ahmed Yusuf, who is serving a life sentence for the 1993 World Trade Center bombing in New York and other terrorist crimes, used his computer to develop a plot to blow up some dozen American airliners over the Pacific.

And terror networks, such as the underground infrastructure of Osama bin Laden, who has been implicated in the US Embassy bombings in Kenya and Tanzania last summer, are sustained via personal computers with satellite uplinks and encrypted messages.

Is the worst yet to come?

Consider waking one morning to the news that a group of terrorists employing electronic "sniffers" have sabotaged the global financial system by disrupting international fund-transfer networks, causing an unprecedented stocks plunge on the New York, London and Tokyo exchanges.

Clearly, there are numerous other devastating scenarios, including altering formulas for medication at pharmaceutical plants; "crashing" telephone systems; misrouting passenger trains; changing pressure in gas pipelines to cause valve failure; disrupting operations of air-traffic control towers; triggering oil refinery explosions and fires; scrambling the software used by emergency services; turning off power grids; and simultaneously detonating hundreds of computerized bombs around the world.

In sum, this new medium of communication, command and control, supplemented by the repeated destructive keyboard attacks on civilian and military nerve centers that we have already seen, forces us to think the unthinkable — and take action to prevent it.

If the expanding electronic perils are ignored by the international community, it is likely that the 21st century could produce a global Waterloo for civilization.

The above articles are just a taste of Y2K and computer related scenarios facing Israel and the world.

There are two men who are experts on this subject, both of whom I greatly admire: Don McAlvany and Chuck Missler. They emphasize these above scenarios and others as Y2K approaches. They emphasize the dislocations that can be expected on and after January 1st, 2000.

Without disputing for a moment their assessments, I am worried about what will happen long before January 1st, 2000. The coming months, I believe will be fateful for Israel and the world. The Islamic countries have imported over a trillion dollars of arms of mass destruction mostly from the US and Russia over the last 26 years. The Syrians alone have over 1,000 missiles (300 Scuds and 700 Frogs) of Soviet manufacture. These missiles can target any place in Israel with a ten-yard accuracy. Since their Scud warheads carry a ton-and-a-quarter payload, that gives each missile the force of the Oklahoma City bombing in which almost 170 people lost their lives. Well, multiply 170 people x 1,000 missiles and the result is a potential catastrophe of 170,000 Israeli casualties within the first minutes of the any such war, within two minutes of each launching.

This helps to explain the Israel Labor Party's security position regarding the need to make peace quickly with Israel's Arab and Islamic (Iranian) neighbors. But the fly in the ointment is that these Soviet-made missiles are Y2K prone. In other words, no one knows how these missiles will function or malfunction on or after January 1st, 2000.

In addition, there are tanks, planes, ships, submarines, artillery and other weapons systems Y2K prone. Israel has virtually solved its Y2K problems, but the Arabs and Russians have not. So either they use it or lose it.

For this reason, among others, my belief is that they will attack Israel before the year 2000. After that war, they believe they can always rearm with Y2K compliant weapons of the next generation. In my first book, I referred to two quotes of Syrian President Hafez Assad. The first was to the effect that the Arabs had lost five wars with Israel. They can afford to lose a sixth war, a seventh war and even the 99th war. All the Arabs need is the 100th war, and there will be no more Israel. The second quote was that the Moslems waited two hundred years to expel the Christian Crusaders from the Middle East. The Jews have only been around 50 years, so the Arabs could wait another 150 years. These two factors in Arab-Islamic thinking give them the feeling of invincibility and that with patience, they can wear out the Jews by wars of attrition. The Arabs-Moslems have never experienced a Holocaust and do not realize the fire they are playing with.

But even if war does not break out in the Middle East before the year 2000, the Islamic demographic trends over the coming years are a cause for concern. The US and Europe are being overrun by Islamic demographic groups which threaten the very Judeo-Christian nature of democracy and civilization in the world as we know it. The strategic balance is turning more and more against Israel with every passing day as the Islamic strength grows in every non-Islamic country. The writing for Israel is on the wall.

In my chapter on the Rise and Fall of American Jewry, I spoke of what I feared in the best case scenario — that there would be attrition and shrinking of the American Jewish communities due to attrition sinking to a low of three million Jews in the US by the year 2015.

But what is the worst case scenario? What happens if a war breaks out in the MIddle East in the near future?

Israel is attacked, because of Y2K, before January 1st, 2000. It is attacked on all fronts simultaneously because Prime Minister Ehud Barak is not capitulating "fast enough" for the Moslems.

The Syrians target our cities before their missiles become obsolete. The Palestinians attack from within with their 50,000 AK-47 machine guns. Fighting is house-to-house in Tel-Aviv, Jerusalem and Petach Tiqva as Palestinian leaders have promised or threatened.

Jordanian, Iraqi and Saudi forces attack from the east. Egypt attacks across the Sinai in direct contravention of the peace agreement.

Israel takes five-digit casualties, God forbid. Israel is faced with one of two alternatives: either losing or winning. The former represents the destruction of Israel while the latter, which honestly is the only alternative, is rolling back the Arab-Islamic armies.

In days, weeks, and maybe even months of terrible battles, Israel finds itself again on the Suez Canal to the West. To the North and East, Israel reaches the Turkish border on the Euphrates River. This will have been the first time in 3,000 years since the reign of King Solomon that Israel's biblically promised borders are realized. Though Damascus is destroyed according to Isaiah 17:1, I personally believe it will be taken in battle and settled by Israel.

Since Israel's population is no longer 3.5 million Jews and Christians as it was until the 1980's, but is now 5 million, Jewish settlement of the new territories will be possible.

Jordan becomes the new home of the those surviving Palestinians fleeing from Judea, Samaria and Gaza after their furtive and futile attempt to destroy Israel from within. Jordan becomes the de facto and de jure Palestinian state.

Israel's victory and survival are received by the world as a burdensome stone and a cup of trembling as it says in Zechariah 12. The world is furious with Israel for daring to win, for daring to survive.

Israel becomes a pariah state, much like Iraq or Serbia. Prime Minister Barak, who was so supported by President Clinton in the elections is now considered worse than Slobodan Milosevic. Barak's crime is that he dared to defend his country and its people. Prime Minister Ehud Barak will be viciously attacked by the world for doing his duty. But Israel will march united. The Likud will be a loyal opposition as it was in 1948, 1956, 1967, 1968-70, and 1973 and unlike Labor which was critical of the Likud's Operation Peace in the Galilee of 1982. There is a reason God chose Barak to be elected at a time such as this.

What about American Jewry? The worst case scenario, I fear, is a tremendous wave of anti-semitism already beginning to crop up in the US. Wall Street will crash with the combination of war in the Middle East, Islamic global terrorism, Y2K and random computer attacks of terrorists and "hackers or crackers." There will be economic dislocation and rioting, with the Jews being the primary target and scapegoat.

Martial law will be declared. Mass detention centers throughout the US already prepared for precisely this contingency will become operational.

Pastor David Wilkerson's prophecy or prediction of the "ghettoes" going up in flames and the attacks on Jews by enraged mobs and minorities will become a reality.

Jews everywhere are scapegoated for the economic chaos in America and the resulting upheaval. True Christians, rising to defend the Jews are persecuted even more than the Jews just as Christians opponents of Adolf Hitler were the first to be eliminated in Nazi Germany even before the Jewish Holocaust went into high gear.

Suddenly, the unthinkable happens. American Jews begin to flee America, and they flee to Israel. It was God's only way to get the Jews home.

Many Jews will be hidden by Christian protectors or "guardian-angels". Those who survive the turning tides against the Jews and Christians will eventually come out of hiding and make their way to Israel. This must include Christians as well. In Isaiah Chapter 60, there is a description of the gentiles bringing home the Jews on their ships. The gentiles also bring their gold and silver. They serve the Lord in Jerusalem. In Zachariah 14, it says that all nations must serve the Lord in Jerusalem. But how can these scriptures be fulfilled if the Christians can't enter the Land?

The doors, that have been closed to Christian immigration begrudgingly begin to open. It says in Genesis and Numbers: Those who bless Israel are blessed. Those who curse Israel are cursed. How can the gentiles bless Israel if Israel doesn't let them? How can they bring home the Jews and not be allowed in themselves? Because of the pariah status of Israel, this situation will change, and the gentiles will be allowed in. Anyone crazy enough to support Israel will be welcomed.

The Israeli population thus grows radically in a very short span of time — from 5 million to 10 million and more within a few years.

Sinai and the new territories toward the Euphrates are massively settled as are the Galilee and Negev. Settlement of Judea, Samaria, and Gaza continue apace.

The world snarls at Israel, hating and boycotting it, yet Israel grows by leaps and bounds in the face of the world. Where there is economic upheaval and convulsions globally, Israel becomes an island of stability in the midst of it all. It says in the Bible that all nations will rise up against Jerusalem. But God, almighty, will manifest Himself in the defense of Jerusalem, in defense of the Jew and Christian.

The "naqba" or disaster of the Palestinian people of 1948 will be nothing compared to the holocaust they will bring upon themselves in this next inevitable war against Israel, the Jews, and the Christians.

Unlike Jews and Christians, the Islamic world has never experienced a holocaust as the Jews have, and have never experienced the futile destruction of hundreds of years of wars between Christians and Christians in Europe. They do not understand peace but only conquest in the name of Allah. This will be the final downfall of Islam, the Koran, and Allah. The only salvation for Moslems is when they abandon the god Allah – a god of the sword and of destruction.

Those who survive must make repentance and serve the Lord, the God of Abraham, Isaac, and Jacob in Jerusalem. The Bible will finally and totally be victorious and bury the Koran — the satanic book of abrogations. Every knee will bend, and every tongue will vow loyalty.

Satanic Islam will be a sad chapter of suffering in world history. All will become followers of the God of Abraham, Isaac and Jacob. All will follow the precepts of love (Deuteronomy 6:4-9; Leviticus 19:18; and Mark 12:28-31). All will await the Jewish Messiah who speaks Hebrew.

At that time, there will be a great family reunion at the food of the Mount of Olives in Jerusalem as we await the great day.

For this, the only answer is Christian Revival for Israel's Survival. Israel's survival includes the survival of the Christian West and the entire world for that matter. Those who bless Israel will be blessed. Those who curse Israel will be cursed.